amuzings!

For the Woodmans!

Thanks for setting me on
the road to wonder.
I've never stopped
exploring!

Also by DWAYNE R. JAMES:

Gingers & Wry

Gingers & Wry
An Illustrated Companion

Obsidian Fire 1:
The Cave of the Sleeping Sword

Obsidian Fire 2:
Revelations of a Secret Brotherhood

Coming Soon-ish:

The Anachronistic Code

For more information on these titles, visit
www.dwaynerjames.com

amuzings

A collection of over 1,100 light-hearted quips, puns, one-liners, & zingers.

DWAYNE R. JAMES

First printing: May 2018
Second printing: June 2018

Copyright © 2018 Dwayne R. James

Printed by CreateSpace, An Amazon.com Company
Available from Amazon.com, CreateSpace.com, and other retail
outlets

ISBN-13: 978-1928015215

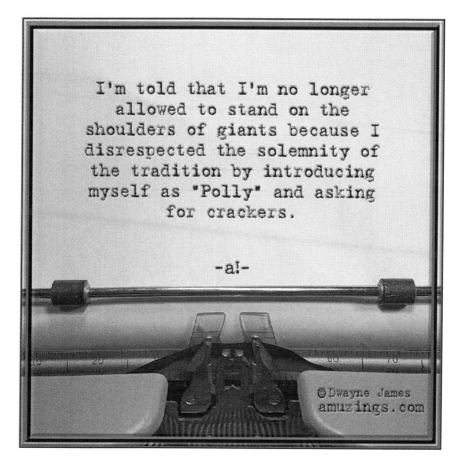

I'm told that I'm no longer allowed to stand on the shoulders of giants because I disrespected the solemnity of the tradition by introducing myself as "Polly" and asking for crackers.

-al-

© Dwayne James
amuzings.com

DEDICATION

Ok, so you're a few pages into my book and already you're wondering why the cover and graphics have typewritten versions of computer-based social media posts. Well, the answer is partly aesthetics in that I thought it looked cool, but also because of my late father.

When Dad died in 2014, the family gathered to go through his possessions. As we sorted through his files, we kept finding these little slips of yellowed paper on which were typewritten notes. The content varied; some were silly poems, or obscure expressions, or adages, or words to live by.

None of us had ever seen these before, except my mother. She told us that when my father had been very young, he would put a few of these slips in his pockets when he went to parties. Then, he would pull them out at random to spice up dying conversations or simply to get a laugh.

Yes. *My father*. Apparently, he used to be the life of the party in his youth.

Now, I can't say I understand his humour, but one thing is clear – he was ahead of his time. By broadcasting his thoughts in public, he was practicing social media long before anybody else!

I don't know if my father would have laughed at this collection of irreverent comments that I've decided to call amuzings, but I'm going to dedicate it to him anyhow, as I attempt to carry on his tradition of trying to inject a little bit of humour into social settings.

I hope you enjoy these little snippets, and I'd like to thank my Dad for, once again, coming up with a great idea for me to emulate.

> Not a day goes by when I'm not grateful to you Dad,
> Dwayne

TABLE OF CONTENTS

TABLE OF CONTENTS, CONT'D

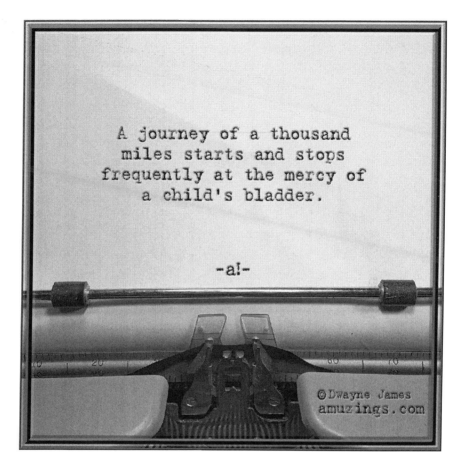

A journey of a thousand miles starts and stops frequently at the mercy of a child's bladder.

-aj-

© Dwayne James
amuzings.com

INTRODUCTION
The Story So Far...

If you're new to the story, let me catch you up on the journey already in progress...

I'm *Dwayne*. I'm an artist and writer, but it wasn't always that way. For many years, I was a single-father for a precocious young girl while I worked from home for a large computer company. Then, things changed.

Literally overnight.

I met an amazing woman and fell head over toes in love. Long story short: in a matter of a year, we were married and expecting twins, but it's the precise manner in which it happened that continues to boggle the mind. As the story goes (and I am NOT making this up), my wife and I found out that she was pregnant with twins the day after I was laid off from the aforementioned good paying job in January of 2009.

The months and years that followed were equal parts challenging and rewarding as I balanced my new role as a stay@home Dad with the excitement of establishing myself as a fledgling artist and all-around creative type. During this dramatic period of my life, one of the things that helped keep me sane was my ability to provide a running commentary on Social Media about the insanity of it all. In 2012, I gathered up all of the posts that I'd made to that point, composed a narrative to link it all together, and self-published it as a book called *Gingers & Wry*.

In the months and years since *G&W* came out, my ginger kids have grown quite a bit. The twins have gone to grade school, my daughter has gone to University, and all three continue to delight and amaze me. As for my wife and me, she's well respected at her job, and I've carved out a comfortable niche in the local arts community.

Through it all, I've continued to post irreverent commentary about life's wonders and absurdities on Social Media. I began to ponder putting the comments into a collection after a few chance meetings with friends in the last month who independently told me how much they enjoyed my sense of humour and would like to see it published. So, if you're looking for somebody to blame for this book, I'll release their names unless they offer me a good reason not too (I'm talking about a bribe here in case that fact isn't abundantly clear enough already).

This collection differs from *G&W* in that it doesn't have the running narrative. It focuses primarily on roughly six years' worth of the quips, puns, one-liners, and zingers that I've come to call *amuzings*. As an added bonus, I've also included two short-stories that I composed originally for two separate iterations of the **CBC Non-Fiction story contest**. Although neither one was recognized in their respective contests, *Lies I Told My Father* was later noticed by a producer on **Stuart Mclean's** *Vinyl Café* Radio program. She had wanted to include it on a future show as a part of the "Stories from Listeners" segment, but it never happened due to Stuart's untimely death in 2017 (Um. Just to be clear. I did not mean to make it sound like I'm complaining that another person's death was inconvenient for me. That's clear, right?)

I also want to point out (because I had a conversation about this recently on Facebook) that all the content in this book is original. Although I don't claim to be the first to have come up with some of these ideas, I can honestly claim that they are all my own unique thoughts. The only person that I've plagiarized is myself in that a handful of the quotes were published previously in *G&W*, and I've used most of the Chapter headings as well since I liked them so much the first time. So, be prepared for a preponderance of the word "Ginger!"

Oh, one last point. I've avoided the use of proper names (aside from my own of course) for reasons of privacy which, I realize, on Facebook is a joke in and of itself. In fact, I *did* write a joke about it, and here it is in the form of a fitting amuzing:

```
Isn't it ironic to join a SOCIAL network and
expect privacy?

Isn't that like going to a party and telling
people that you're not really there?
```

One last comment: I'm not convinced that there's a good way to read the content of this book because it's not necessarily designed to be read from start to finish. I've broken it up into sections and sub-sections with the idea that you can flip to any part of the book and read a few pages and walk away amused as well as satisfied that you can do the same thing all over again later. With over 1,100 amuzings and stories to choose from, I'm confident that you'll be hard pressed to repeat yourself anytime soon!

Happy reading!

-a!-

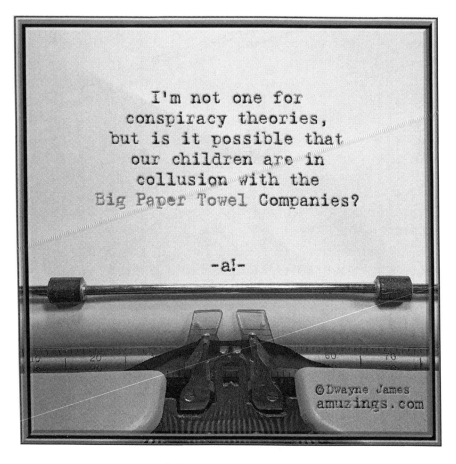

I'm not one for
conspiracy theories,
but is it possible that
our children are in
collusion with the
Big Paper Towel Companies?

-a!-

©Dwayne James
amuzings.com

GINGER TALES
Keeping It In The Family

My sons were very excited when I told them that
we had a time machine in the house until I told
them it was a clock.

-a!-

Ah. The pitter patter of little feet chasing
each other around the house. Also, screaming.

-a!-

So far at our Yard Sale, it's been profitable
with the boys buying back their toys with the
profits from their bake sale.

-a!-

It only took my sons a half hour to figure out
how to play their new recorders with their
noses.

I'm so proud I could just spit.

-a!-

We're thinking of having hot-oil fondue for
supper tonight with the boys.

I wonder if we can call the hospital E.R. ahead
of time and make a reservation.

-a!-

Apparently, my wife has yet to master the art of
catching a spider in front of children, because
she just said, "Whoops. Where'd it go?"

-a!-

Twins.

Because repeating yourself six times every time
you give an order to one child just wasn't quite
taxing enough.

-a!-

When somebody yells to me from another room, I
like to answer quietly in gibberish.

Inevitably, after they reply with, "I can't hear
you, you're in another room," I'll answer,
"Exactly."

-a!-

My sons: making me doubt whether or not I'm
actually speaking out loud since 2009.

-a!-

In this technological age, one of the most
dangerous things in your kid's hand is a magnet.

"Look Dad! It sticks to the TV!"

-a!-

Having sons, it's never clearer why it's called
"boisterous" and not "girlsterous."

-a!-

Me, as I'm walking out of my twins' room after
putting them to bed and they ask for water:
"Just when I thought I was out, they pull me
back in!"

-a!-

The excitement of being served breakfast in bed
this morning is somewhat mitigated by the
discovery that the boys served it on plates
directly from a dirty dishwasher.

-a!-

So, we're down to 1.5 pairs of mittens, with the
last complete pair being caught in a temporal
flux as it only makes occasional appearances.

-a!-

The frikkin' "looking with fingers" phase that
all little boys go through ends eventually,
right? Right?

-a!-

Dear Mom, you spoil my righteous indignation
every time you say, "I know exactly how that
feels" whenever I complain about having to clean
up after messy boys.

-a!-

How early is it in the school year?

Well, I haven't started wearing pajamas to drop
the kids off at the bus stop yet, so that's
saying something.

-a!-

My mother just told me that there was a stupid
fly bothering her.

"Would you prefer to be bothered by a smart fly
instead?" I asked her.

I swear, sometimes, she can be such an elitist.

-a!-

Children.

They're the reason you have to resort to duct
taping the remote to the coffee table to keep it
from going missing.

-a!-

I'm just saying that I have high standards for
kid's TV.

If *Tinky-Winky* is going to chase a ball, I want
to know WHY. What's his motivation?

-a!-

Nothing makes me recoil in fear quite like the
phrase, "Here Daddy, smell this."

-a!-

Best April Fool's joke on me was by the raccoon
who, finding the compost lid
uncharacteristically unsecured, simply ran off
with the it.

I'm calling it. *The raccoon wins!*

-a!-

If I've learned one thing from having kids, it's
that even when you have a plan, you don't really
have a plan.

-a!-

Earlier, I found out that when rushing to help a
puking child, watch for the other child rushing
just as fast to get away from that puke.

-a!-

Earlier tonight, I was baking cookies when my
Aunt voiced the concern that my raw cookies were
too close together, and would run all together
in the oven.

"Of course they will," I answered. "I'm using a
cookie sheet. If I wanted to bake more than one
cookie, I would need to use a *cookies* sheet."

-a!-

These kids aren't just one-derful, they're
twin-derful!

-a!-

So, glass half full: none of my kids are
destined to be serial killers, as none of them
can clean up after themselves!

-a!-

I desperately want to ask my sons if they
flushed my missing car key, but fear it might
give them ideas that the toilet isn't just for
flushing things like the meals that Daddy
ruined.

-a!-

Kids: when breaking all your own stuff yourself
just isn't feasible.

-a!-

The man who covers his crotch protectively when
his kids jump into bed with him in the morning
has learned his lesson.

-a!-

I get way too amused every time one of my kids
comes back in the room saying, "You were wrong
Daddy. Mommy wasn't calling me."

-a!-

I swear, one day, at least one of my kids will
understand that I'm being sarcastic when I say,
"I don't know where your stuffy is; I don't
recall where I left it when last I played with
it."

-a!-

Somebody in my extended family just shared that
viral post about how sad it is when family
members feud with each other.

I'd agree with her, but unfortunately, we're not
on speaking terms.

-a!-

I just realized that, 9 times out of 10, when I
say, "Thank you for listening" to my sons, I'm
being sarcastic.

-a!-

Say what you want about how nice my MOM is.

But if she really was the "saint" you think she
is, she'd have told me by now where we bought
the self-cleaning toilets in my childhood home.

-a!-

TOILET TRAUMA

I'd heard of the expression "top of the morning", but didn't know what the bottom of the morning was until I changed my first newborn at 3AM.

-a!-

Apparently nothing makes a child need to poo more desperately than a toilet that is already occupied.

-a!-

Y'know what would be honesty in advertising?

Naming a brand of snowsuits for kids "laxative suits", because nothing makes a toddler need to poo more than putting on a snowsuit.

-a!-

Caught my son standing on top of his play house peeing in the bush while singing.

Naturally, I'm now calling him "The Piddler on the Roof."

-a!-

When an infant fills a diaper forcefully enough to break the sound barrier, it is called a sonic boom-boom.

-a!-

RAISING GIRLS IS JUST EASIER...

Every once in a while, I text my teenaged
daughter during the day.

When she responds, I tell her to stop texting in
school.

-a!-

Tonight, one of my daughter's teenaged male
friends asked me what my first name was.

"Mister," I answered.

-a!-

My daughter misheard something I said today, and
it is now my new favourite expression.

She heard, "This is crazier than a moose
festival!"

-a!-

I asked my daughter how it was watching the boys
today while my wife and I were out.

"I've seen things..." she replied through a
vacant stare.

Sounds about right.

-a!-

My daughter is now safely home from her trip to
India.

She's walking around a little dazed now,
something that I think has a lot to do with the
twelve hour time difference. Or, maybe it's the
decided lack of cows in our yard.

It could go either way.

HAVING KIDS MEANS...

Having kids means accepting the fact that the phrase, "Give me a second," ceases to have any meaning whatsoever.

-a!-

Having kids is basically repeating, "I don't know where your <item> is" and trying, sometimes unsuccessfully, not to modify it with the word "fucking."

-a!-

Having kids is never being able to laugh out loud again without being asked to explain what's so funny, and then being told it wasn't funny.

-a!-

Having kids means engaging in regular semantical "discussions" over the difference between playing with something and simply touching it.

-a!-

Having kids is never, ever really knowing for sure who had the toy first.

-a!-

Having kids means putting the word C-A-N-D-Y on par with "He who must not be named."

-a!-

Having kids is buying expensive water-proof mittens for some stranger's kid to wear when yours loses them at school.

-a!-

Having kids is like the scene from Last Crusade
when Indy picks a grail, only it's "One of the
cups had kid spit in it, and you chose poorly."

-a!-

TO HAVE AND TO HOLD
AND TWO HALVES MAKE A WHOLE...

My wife just told me that she's pregnant.

Surely there is a less stressful way for her to check to see if I'm paying attention.

-a!-

"I can't believe the dishes we have," said my wife.

"Why?" I asked. "Do you think they're lying to you about something?"

-a!-

Today, at our yard sale, my wife said, "I can't believe it's so cold."

"Really," I responded sardonically. "It's twelve degrees Celsius and you're shivering. What more proof do you need?"

She can be such a skeptic at times.

-a!-

Apparently, saying, "But my Mom always let me have some," is NOT the best way to get your wife to give you raw dough while she's baking.

-a!-

My wife just told me not to touch the gingerbread dough.

If *Mission Impossible* has taught me anything, there's a loophole here somewhere.

-a!-

Whenever I can't find something, I really must
learn to stop saying, "I defy you to find it,"
to my wife when she takes up the cause.

-a!-

This morning, my wife said, "The next time you
want to know where something is, just ask me to
show you."

My imagination is awash with the possibilities.

-a!-

Advice I gave my wife this morning as she walked
down the icy path towards our garage: "I'm
filming you, so if you fall, do it hilariously
so this video goes viral."

-a!-

My wife just asked me to turn the kettle on.

Perhaps I'll start with some erotic literature.
I suspect that the slow-burn variety will be
most appropriate.

-a!-

I've finally upgraded my drill after many years
to celebrate my new workshop.

Today, I found my wife trying to put a screw in
the wall using a screwdriver, and it wasn't
going well since the screw was going in crooked.

"Having problems?" I asked. "Want to use my new
drill?"

"Why? Will it drive it straight?"

"No," I replied. "It'll still go in crooked.
It'll just go in MUCH faster."

-a!-

While my wife was cleaning out the fridge yesterday she said, "There's left-over pie in here. Did you know that?"

"Not to appear sarcastic dear," I replied as sweetly as I could. "But I think it's pretty obvious that, if I KNEW that there was left-over pie in the fridge, there wouldn't BE any left-over pie in the fridge."

-a!-

This morning, I found my toothpaste tube empty when I went to brush my teeth.

Speaking to the tube, I said, "I find your lack of paste disturbing."

My wife no longer shares the washroom with me during our morning toiletries.

-a!-

My wife just texted me to say she was going back to the office to check out a few thongs.

Sure, but when I do it...

-a!-

I've learned that, when someone is in a really grouchy mood, saying, "Good morning Oscar" just makes things worse.

-a!-

This morning, my wife told me she was going to strip the bed.

"How fortuitous," I said, "'The bed' just happens to be my nick-name."

-a!-

As a good husband, I like to ask my wife if
there's anything I can help with before I bolt
from the room, so at least I can say that I
asked.

-a!-

I must remember to ask my wife where she got the
mug that she gave me for my birthday. I'd like
to go back and get one for me too.

-a!-

You know darn well when, at 7AM on a cold
morning, your wife says that "we need to go out
and get some milk" that she doesn't really mean
"we".

-a!-

OTHER MARRIAGE CONTRACTS

Every marriage should have access to waivers and contracts to be used when appropriate.

Like this one for instance:

I, the wife, acknowledge that, in undertaking this simple project on my behalf, you, the husband, reserve the right to grossly OVERCOMPLICATE said simple project.

I, the wife, also agree to return all tools (power and otherwise) that I have formerly confiscated, even though their use may not immediately or obviously be related to the new endeavour in question.

Further, lest we risk a repeat of the unfortunate "I can't find the car keys" incident of 2012, I, the wife, agree to have the vehicle ready for a quick trip to the hospital should said project require the use of any of the following implements of minor destruction: blow-torch, chainsaw, nail-gun, industrial-strength adhesive, cheesecloth, extra sharp box-cutter, and/or step ladder.

-a!-

A HOUSE-HUSBAND'S WORK IS NEVER DONE...

A reproduction of today's House-husbandly TODO list:

1. Clean washrooms.

2. Make a big deal about me having cleaned washrooms.

Looks like I'm pretty much done here.

-a!-

If the first thing your wife says when she gets home from work is "What's that smell?", chances are the supper you made is not going to be well received.

-a!-

BOYS WILL BREAK THINGS...

This weekend, my sons asked me to build them a teeter-totter, and naturally, I got to thinking about the one that I built with my brother when I was maybe 9 or 10.

First, you have to understand that my father had a lot of wood, what with being a carpenter and all, but there was only one piece of wood that he held above all others: his prized 12 foot long 2 by 10. He'd had this particular piece of wood for years, and used it on scaffolding because, being roughly milled, it was so thick that it could easily support the weight of a full-grown man.

Anyhow, one summer when he was at work, my brother and I took this prized piece of lumber, balanced it across the peak of the dog house, took our places on either end, and started using it as a teeter-totter. It didn't take us long to discover that when one of us dropped to the ground really quickly, the person on the other end of the piece of wood would be sent sailing up into the air before eventually slamming back down onto the end of the plank.

As young boys, this amused us to no end, and we began to compete to see how high we could each throw the other. We were having a ball, until, on the return trip from a particularly good toss in which one of us had almost reached escape velocity, our combined weight on the extreme ends of the board of wood snapped it cleanly in half over the back of the doghouse.

Luckily, we didn't get hurt, and quickly set about trying to hide the broken lumber from my father, as he was due home any minute.

Of course, it didn't take him long to find the two remaining pieces of his once mighty board, and he was understandably upset. One could say livid.

"Who in the hell broke my piece of wood?!" he bellowed from the garage, before pausing for a moment in thought as the all-important follow-up question occurred to him: "HOW in the hell did you break my piece of wood?"

It's because of stories like this that I realize that my boys come by their affinity for breaking things honestly.

It helps me keep perspective, if not my patience.

-a!-

QUESTIONABLE INSTRUCTIONS

Please note that my mother's most recent book "How to Melt Butter in your Son's Microwave" contained the following errors:

In *Step 3*, you should put the butter in a BOWL and not on a PLATE as instructed.

In *Step 6*, please set the microwave for 10 SECONDS and not 10 MINUTES as listed.

Lastly the final step was omitted from this publication, and should read:

Step 12: Should the butter overflow the container, please clean your son's microwave before his wife sees it and blames him for it.

We apologize for any inconvenience that these mistakes may have caused.

-a!-

QUESTIONABLE PARENTING

In retrospect, telling my daughter not to bother
closing the door to the scary furnace room (the
room right beside her bedroom) as "it always
opens up by itself anyway", was a mistake.

-a!-

In retrospect, perhaps I shouldn't have asked my
sons if they were concerned that wearing glow in
the dark pajamas would make it easier for the
monsters to find them.

-a!-

My son is blocking the door and won't let me
through until I give him the correct password.

I'm not sure, but I don't think "Get the hell
out of my way you little shit" is what he's
looking for.

-a!-

Putting the boys to bed tonight, I told them
that every time they got up when they were
supposed to be sleeping, I got to eat one of
their advent calendar chocolates.

"So, please get up lots," I said. "I love those
chocolates."

They told me that they understood, but just a
few short minutes later, I heard one of them
asking for a glass of water.

"Ok, c'mon to the kitchen and get it," I said.

"Wait," I heard the other boy say. "It might be
a trap! He wants our chocolate!"

Smart kid.

Maybe I'll share some of his chocolate with him.

-a!-

Gotta remember not to use gas to light the
campfire when the boys are watching, because now
they're like, "Daddy, make it go WHOOSH again!"
and I'm like, "Not until my eyebrows grow back."

-a!-

Posted on my daughter's Facebook timeline:

You got a parcel in the mail today. I didn't
open it, but it feels a lot like a hash pipe.

We should talk.

-a!-

So, apparently, handing a single toy to your
twin sons and sarcastically telling them to
loudly fight over it is not "effective
parenting."

-a!-

ON THREE-YEAR OLDS

My wife explaining the flu to my three-year old
son: "You were sick last summer because you had
a bug in your tummy."

"Oh," he replied. "Was it a bee?"

-a!-

Overheard earlier: a huge crashing sound from
the living room followed by the tiny voice of a
child saying, "Yep, it gonna fall."

-a!-

Apparently, my three-year old boys still aren't
clear on the concept of putting garbage out on
the curb for pick-up.

Earlier today, they were yelling out the window
at the recycling truck after it had finished at
our house, loudly saying, "No go 'way wif
Daddy's stuff!"

-a!-

Y'know, when the twins ask for a drink, I might
just as well pour it on the floor immediately
since that's where it ends up anyway.

-a!-

There are some mornings when it would be easier
to go out on the parkway and put the twins'
clothes on the cars as they speed by.

-a!-

Something else I'd never thought I'd ever have
to say until I had kids: "Please don't lick the
car."

-a!-

"Why, yes son, there is a 'big, big clock' up
there on the tower.

Now, what say we use our inside voices while
we're out in public, and how about we also teach
you how to pronounce the letter 'L'."

-a!-

This morning at breakfast, my son announced, "My
tummy saying something."

"What is it saying?" I asked.

"It saying thank you for breakfast."

I'm so grateful that I'm raising such grateful
children

-a!-

And tonight's Eureka moment is from my eldest
son who, while holding his crotch and shifting
uncomfortably from one foot to the other
declared, "Mommy, me think drinking water make
me pee."

-a!-

I try to help out in the morning, but the boys
only want their Mommy brushing their teeth and
getting them dressed.

"Is there anything I can do?" I asked my son
exasperated.

"Mommy?" he offered.

"Well, I'll ask," I answered under my breath.
"But I don't think she'll go for it. She has to
get to work."

-a!-

I'll be honest. I'd be a little happier if just half the bums I wiped each day were mine.

-a!-

Earlier this morning, my youngest son wanted to play on the floor.

"Daddy," he requested. "Lie on your back."

"OK," I replied as I got down on the floor on my back. "I have a full head of hair, and I voted Conservative in the last election."

-a!-

Nothing strikes fear in the heart of a parent quite like hearing the phrase, "Look Daddy, I can fly."

-a!-

Where I'd like to take it as a compliment when the boys tell me "you weally funny", I've also heard them say the same thing about the Wiggles.

-a!-

I love that the sentences and phrases that the twins come out with are getting more and more complicated even though they don't always make sense.

Just now, for example, as I threw a comforter over his head while we were putting him to bed, my youngest exclaimed, "Hey! Who somebody turned light outs?"

-a!-

I know we'll have to correct the boys eventually, but for now it's just so cute to hear them say "twenty-ten" instead of "thirty".

-a!-

Overheard in the living room where my wife is
teaching the boys math:

"If you have three apples, and she takes one,
how many do you have left?"

"Wait," protested a tiny voice. "Why she take my
apples?"

-a!-

Yesterday afternoon, my eldest son fell asleep
on the living room floor.

Later, I was playing with his younger twin in
the bedroom when he asked where his brother was.

"He's having a cat-nap," I answered.

"He no cat, Daddy," replied my son matter-of-
factly. "He having a boy-nap!"

-a!-

Dear sons, where I appreciate you telling me how
much you like the lunch I made you, I'm hurt
that you sound surprised that it's so good.

-a!-

I love what the boys do when they want to tell
me a secret.

They put their ear right in front of my mouth
and start whispering.

-a!-

So, apparently, the only thing that makes a
toddler need to poo more than snowpants, is a
toilet that you're in the middle of cleaning.

-a!-

I just heard one of the boys in the bathtub
yell, "Something touched me!!"

Cue the *Jaws* theme music.

-a!-

My wife just got back from a truncated walk with
the boys, ready to sell a truculent twin for
medical experiments.

Earlier, she asked why I didn't want to go with
them, and why I didn't take the boys for more
walks during the week.

I love it when her questions answer themselves.

-a!-

So, let me get this straight.

My youngest son will pretend that his brother's
foot is a phone so that he can talk to Grandma &
Grandpa, but he'll draw the line at using it to
have a conversation with a cow because "cows
don't talk Daddy."

-a!-

Yesterday, I was continuing the effort to teach
the boys how to tell time by using the clock on
the kitchen wall as a teaching aid.

"Where is the big hand?" I asked them.

Without hesitation, my eldest son pointed
excitedly towards the clock. "Right there," he
replied in a voice that I swear had a sarcastic
tone to it.

-a!-

It's the end of an era.

I grabbed my youngest son's nose earlier and pretended to steal it.

"I've got your nose!" I announced mockingly as I wiggled my thumb between my first and second fingers for him to see.

He narrowed his eyes as he looked up at me then, touching his nose, he replied, "My nose still here Daddy!"

I suppose it's only a matter of time before he figures out that I don't store my pocket change in his ears either.

-a!-

Earlier, the twins were fighting over a shared resource in their bedroom. I placated them by telling them that, one day, they could both have their own room. Now they're arguing over who gets Mommy and Daddy's bedroom.

I don't think they understand how this works.

-a!-

At lunch today, the boys asked if baby carrots tasted the same as their larger counterparts.

"Baby carrots are the same," I answered. "They just taste more innocent."

-a!-

My son just flushed the toilet while saying, "Bye bye mine poo. I'll see you later!"

Really? Does he know something I don't know?

-a!-

While we were giving the boys a bath today, my eldest son picked up the facecloth and started pretending that it was a puppet.

"Hello," he said in a high voice, while moving his thumb to make it look like the puppet's mouth was moving.

"Hello," I replied. "What's your name?"

He looked at me for a moment, and then back at his puppet. When he finally replied through the puppet, it was in a tone of voice that suggested that his answer was an obvious one.

"My hand," said the puppet.

-a!-

What is it with these boys and bodily fluids, and why do I have to keep getting up close and personal with them?

Today, while I was making lunch, my youngest didn't make it to the toilet in time, and peed all over the floor of the bathroom. While I was getting something to clean it up, his brother came tearing around the corner, slipped in the puddle, and fell on his head.

So there I was, hugging two wailing boys, both of them soaked in urine, one of which was asking me to kiss the injured parts of his body that were now covered in his brother's pee.

There is not enough soap in the world to make me feel clean ever again.

-a!-

ON FOUR-YEAR OLDS...

My four-year old son just said, "My penis is boring me."

I don't think he understood it when I replied, "Give it a few years."

-a!-

My sons just ran by, and one said, "You can't catch me 'cause I'm not wearing pants!"

I hope criminals don't discover this escape clause.

-a!-

I need someone that I can call the next time I'm tempted to take the boys shopping so that they can talk me out of it.

-a!-

I like the way this kid thinks.

When asked for a word that starts with "A", my youngest answered, "A cake?"

-a!-

The boys have been learning the national anthem. According to them, Canada is our "gnome and native land" that is "obvious and free".

-a!-

Yesterday, the boys asked me where the holes in Swiss cheese come from.

Dunno if they believed me when I said, "The very hungry caterpillar."

-a!-

Earlier, the DJ said, "I'm just going to throw
this out there," and my four-year old responded,
"That man gonna throw something out the radio!"

-a!-

This morning, as I headed out to scrape the
snow-encrusted van, my four-year old asked,
"Daddy, you gonna shave the car?"

-a!-

It's called "Nutella" son. Please don't call it
"Chocolate Spread" in front of Mommy, or you'll
weaken our case to have it for breakfast.

-a!-

TODDLER TIME:

The time on your clock radio, unique from the
actual time, because your toddler has been
playing with the time-set buttons.

-a!-

Overheard earlier: "Mommy say that fart and shit
be bad words."

Apparently, the boys and I are going to have to
have a little talk.

In the first place, that grammar is completely
unacceptable, and secondly, why is Mommy always
the authority figure?

-a!-

ON FIVE-YEAR OLDS

We stumbled across an Abbot and Costello comedy routine while the boys were telling me about the French Alphabet.

"Igrec?" I asked after they had finished rhyming the letters off. "That sounds like the name for a bird. What letter is that?"

"Y," answered my youngest son.

"Because I want to know," I replied smugly.

Hilarity ensued once they understood the play on words.

-a!-

My sons have added a new component to rock, paper, scissors: puke.

I'm no expert, but I'm pretty sure that wins every time.

-a!-

As a father of twin boys, I was honestly completely unprepared for the sheer number of times I'd be asking, "Why are you naked?"

-a!-

My five-year old son woke us up with a joke this morning.

"Why is 6 afraid of 7?" He asked.

"Because 6, 7, 8," he finished.

Somehow, it's funnier his way.

-a!-

My sons just signed all of their Valentine's day
cards. I must say, they have excellent
penboyship.

-a!-

Earlier today, my son asked me why I was buying
printer paper.

"Can't we just put a page on the scanner and
make some copies of it?" he asked.

-a!-

This morning, just a few days after Christmas,
we overheard our sons in the kitchen trying to
decide what to serve us for our breakfast in
bed.

"How about gingerbread house?" one of them said.

Beside me, my wife tensed. "Honey...." she
groaned into her pillow. "Can you go help them?"

"No, wait," I replied. "I want to see where they
go with this."

-a!-

ON SIX-YEAR OLDS...

My six-year old son, upon discovering what
happens when you shake a bottle of pop before
opening it: "Daddy! I just made science!"

-a!-

The boys were playing shadow puppets. Naturally,
the soundtrack I provided was: "I see a little
silhouette of a hand..."

-a!-

"Mommy, why are you wearing earplugs?" asked my
youngest son tonight.

"So I don't hear your yelling," Mommy answered
wearily.

"Can I have some earplugs too?" he begged. "I
don't want to hear my yelling either."

-a!-

Overheard in the living room just now:

SMACK!

"OWWW!"

"There was a fly on your bum."

Somehow, even I doubt there was really a fly on
his bum.

-a!-

Overheard in the twins' bedroom earlier: "Will
you please keep your toots under the blanket!"

Well, at least he was polite about it.

-a!-

Today I was playing rocket ship with the boys
during which they pretended to be space bunnies
who ate the sun.

Apparently, it was a nice light snack.

-a!-

Thanks to my sons' new lightsaber toothbrushes,
I've come to realize that the only thing missing
from our bed-time routine was the ability to do
battle.

-a!-

Earlier, I overheard my sons talking about my
new painting.

"He's doing a really good job," one said. "Look
how he's staying in all the lines!"

-a!-

According to my son, the biggest household
hazard for a child isn't a wall receptacle or a
hot stove, but a discarded poppy on the floor.

That pin is the sharpest object known to
humankind.

-a!-

ON SEVEN-YEAR OLDS...

I must remember to teach my kids that, if they
don't know the right answer on tests, they
should write something funny that I can turn
into an internet meme.

-a!-

I know that insanity is expecting different
results from repetition, so why do I still
expect my seven-year olds to use a ketchup
bottle responsibly?

-a!-

As my kids did their homework, I asked, "What's
the French word for 'encore' again?"

Nobody laughed. Tough crowd.

-a!-

On the way to the school bus this morning, we
passed a neighbour.

"It's our birthday," announced my twin sons
cheerily.

"Oh wow!" answered the man-whose-name-I've-
already-forgotten. "You're growing up so fast. I
hardly recognize you from last week, when I met
you for the first time."

Well played, man-whose-name-I've-already-
forgotten. Well played.

-a!-

The first of today's P.A. day messes: picking up
Mommy's high heel shoes where they were
discarded after what appears to have been a
race.

-a!-

Day one of summer vacation with the twins, and I
only raised my voice once: when I caught them
feeding the hose into the van through an open
window to clean its insides.

-a!-

My son's first impression of Ikea: "Everything
here is so fake!"

-a!-

ON EIGHT-YEAR OLDS

Eight-year boys who hang onto the garage door
and ride it while the motor pulls it up are one
of the reasons we can't have nice things.

-a!-

This morning, we found our youngest son hiding
in the corner of his room, changing out of the
PJs that he'd worn to bed the night before.

"Why are you putting on new PJs?" my wife asked.

He looked at us in thought for a moment before
finally answering, "It's complicated."

I have never wanted to know what happened more
than I did right then.

-a!-

My eldest son wants to build a lair out of snow.

Yeah, I'm pretty sure I'm raising a supervillain.

-a!-

Why do I wear shoes in the house?

Because I live with two eight-year old boys, and
the water I slip in on the floor isn't always
water.

-a!-

Today, I was asked how old my sons were when
they first ate solid food.

"That depends," I answered. "Does their own poo
qualify as solid?"

-a!-

The song I sing for my kids when they're getting
ready for bed:

"Brusha brusha brusha brusha, brusha your teeth,

Not too soft, not too hard, but somewhere in
betweeth."

-a!-

My sons are jumping down the staircase onto
pillows at its base.

Should I book a spot in the E.R. ahead of time
or just play it by ear?

-a!-

I'm told that, after tonight's supper, my
approval rating among eight-year olds has hit an
all-time low.

I'm not worried. They're not my target
demographic anyway.

-a!-

Yesterday, my son came in from playing outside
and said, "I went to bad-idea land, Daddy."

"Where?" I asked.

"Bad-idea land," he answered as he sloshed in
through the door. "I wore my snow boots into the
water."

Luckily, I got to him before he could walk
across the carpet in his overflowing, muddy
boots but really, how could I have been angry
when he introduced his actions in such a cute
way?

-a!-

Note to self: next road trip, "forget" my son's recorder at home.

Or along the highway. Either one works.

-a!-

Note to self: when you are emptying a cup of your son's pee out the window of a moving vehicle, be prepared for blowback.

Anyone got a wet nap?

-a!-

My sons were bickering earlier today and I really wanted to intervene.

Not to stop them, mind you, but to correct their grammar.

-a!-

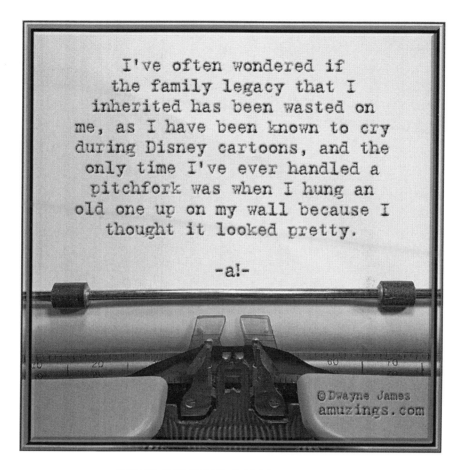

I've often wondered if the family legacy that I inherited has been wasted on me, as I have been known to cry during Disney cartoons, and the only time I've ever handled a pitchfork was when I hung an old one up on my wall because I thought it looked pretty.

-al-

© Dwayne James
amuzings.com

LIES I TOLD MY FATHER
Not Your Average Fish Tale

The following is the eulogy that I read at my father's funeral service in 2014:

I'm Dwayne. I'm Winston's middle child. That should be everything you need to know ahead of time.

As many of you know, I like to tell stories. This eulogy is based heavily on one that I wrote about Dad two years ago, so much of it is written in the present tense.

Here it is:

Last week, my wife discovered a tiny leak in the plumbing in our basement, so I immediately called my father—a former contractor—to ask him how I could repair it myself. He happily obliged, and described the process to me in great detail over the phone. Armed with this information, along with what I was subsequently able to discover for myself on the Internet once I'd put down the phone, I figured that I was all set.

That all changed however when my father called back a short while later to say, "Tell you what. I'll come over this weekend, and *help* you with it."

And there it was.

I'm not sure if my father is unique in this respect, but his concept of the word *help* has always been tenuous at best. I say this with the greatest affection, but that man has never in his life played the role of the *helper*.

Sure enough, it's a few days later, and he's standing on a stepstool in my basement doing the actual work, while I've been relegated to the role of operating-room nurse, handing him tools as he calls for them.

"Emery cloth," he asks, his voice muffled by virtue of the fact that his head is buried in the suspended ceiling.

"Check," I reply while passing it to him.

"Flux."

"Is this what's inside the flux capacitor?" I ask cheekily as I offer up the container. He looks down at me questioningly, eyes narrowed.

Ah yes, I remind myself. *Dad doesn't speak 'geek'.*

Ignoring my comment, he continues, "Hand me the blowtorch and unwind a length of solder."

I give him the torch. He lights it, adjusts the flame, and raises it up above his head to heat the copper pipe. He's swaying unsteadily on the stool, so I press my hand into the small of his back to support him. After a few minutes, he reaches up with the solder in his other hand to melt it against the now hot pipe. I can see that he's having a difficult time trying to keep his hands from shaking, and I'm genuinely concerned that it's causing him to miss the spot that he's supposed to be soldering.

Internally, I'm wondering if our house insurance is paid up, and if the coverage would still apply if a house fire was caused by a blowtorch-wielding madman.

I suppose I should tell you that my father has Parkinson's.

Although it's been a persistent challenge for him since he was diagnosed fifteen years ago, his doctors are amazed at how well he continues to manage his symptoms, all things considered. It helps, I'm sure, that the man is singularly determined, unabashedly stubborn, and absolutely refuses to let somebody else do something that he can damn well do himself.

Yeah, Dad's a tough nut.

Raised on a depression-era farm in the Almonte area of Ontario, he inherited his tough-as-nails attitude from my grandfather, who I'm told once killed a deer with a pitchfork because he didn't have time to go home and get his gun.

This is the family legacy I inherited, even though I often wonder if it's wasted on me, as I have been known to cry during Disney cartoons, and the only time I've ever handled a pitchfork was when I hung an old one up on my wall because I thought it looked pretty.

At 45, I'm finally in a good place with my father. Still, I've always felt like I disappointed him by not being manly enough to truly appreciate his one great passion: *fishing*.

Oh, I had my reasons. For one, I was a fairly sensitive child, and hated having to watch our day's catch slowly asphyxiate to death as it flopped around on the ice while its blood turned the snow around it into a soupy scarlet slush. Nor did I enjoy having to bait my hook by thrusting a sharp point up under a minnow's chin and out through the top of its tiny head.

Blech.

So, apparently I'm a fairly sensitive adult too.

But Dad loved fishing, and who was I to try and convince him otherwise? So I spent my childhood either faking my enthusiasm for it, or outright lying to him about it. Eventually, this charade led to one of the biggest lies I ever told him.

I was in University at the time, home for the holidays. Dad was still teaching, and invited me on an ice fishing trip that his Haliburton high school had organized. I was obviously hesitant, but ultimately came to realize that it represented an excellent opportunity for some quality father/son bonding. At least as long as I didn't actually *catch* anything, and I was pretty confident how I could make sure of that.

Out on the frozen lake a few days later, our rented ice shack was positively luxurious. In fact, it was bigger than my first house—and better insulated too. Once we'd settled in, Dad handed me my kit and pointed to our bucket of minnows.

"You need a refresher?" he teased. He didn't actually call me *city-slicker*, but it was definitely implied.

I laughed and said, "Naw, I'm good," as I reached in and fished out a live minnow. I could feel its tiny body wriggling helplessly in my hand, and I shuddered involuntarily. Then, turning my back to my father, I mimicked the act of lobotomizing the bait, and swiftly dropped the un-tethered minnow down the hole, followed almost immediately by the bare—now impotent—hook.

Giggling at my own impertinence, I settled onto the bench knowing that, since I obviously couldn't catch a fish without bait, I wouldn't have to kill anything today, and my father would never be the wiser. I put my feet up on a stool, leaned back, and asked Dad how his final year of teaching had been going.

It was a couple of hours, and several liberated minnows later, when the unthinkable happened.

As I watched in raw disbelief, my rod dipped suddenly and, might I add, very enthusiastically towards the water, indicating that something—presumably a fish—was pulling on the other end of the line.

Naturally, I immediately assumed that Dad was somehow behind it. After all, this was the same man who, on non-ice fishing trips in my childhood, had frequently tried to fool me into thinking I had a bite by jerking on the line at end of my fishing rod when I wasn't looking.

But that had always been in a canoe, not from a hole in the ice eight feet away!

"Impossible," I muttered. "I can't possibly have a fish." But, as I pulled on the line, the earnest tug that I received by way of a reply was a clear and unequivocal indication to the contrary.

In retrospect, I'm not at all sure what happened next. It was like some kind of primeval urge kicked in, and I began pulling at the line like my life depended on it. Where I had come into this adventure not wanting to kill anything, a switch had been thrown in my brain, and I was suddenly bloodthirsty.

The creature that I eventually pulled up through the opening in the ice was easily the biggest fish I'd ever caught. It barely seemed to fit up through the hole, and I knew that, even as its head towered imperiously over the ice, its tail was stretching deep into the abyss beneath us.

Inexplicably, I wanted that fish, so I put all of my strength into one final tug on the line, and watched horror struck as the hook slipped out of the monster's gill slit where it had been wedged. Amazingly, this unlucky fish hadn't actually tried to bite the hook, it had just happened to snag it as it swam by!

For a moment, the behemoth and I locked eyes, both of us realizing simultaneously that it was free. Then, it began to move — but so did I.

I suppose I could have let it go. With my back to my father, I could have pushed it down the hole in much the same way that I'd freed the minnows, but I was still being ruled by my animalistic alter-ego. Somewhere deep within me, my reptilian brain was rationalizing that, if the universe was letting me catch a fish without using bait, then dammit, the universe *wanted* me to have that fish.

So, with one smooth motion I reached down with both hands, grabbed the squirming fish behind the gills, and hoisted it up over my head triumphantly.

Dad cursed as the fish splashed him, but I could see him smiling. He hadn't caught a fish of his own, but he was obviously having the time of his life watching me catch mine. I feel obliged to add that he did that a lot whenever we went fishing, as I was always the better fisherman. Seriously. I have the pictures to prove it too.

Back in the present, Dad's cursing too. He's just noticed that his blowtorch is melting some ABS piping. Upstairs, my wife has noticed the acrid smell, and has just come down to check on us.

Quietly she asks me, "Should we call a plumber?"

I don't want to tell her in front of Dad that I'd been considering the same thing myself. "It's either that or the fire department," I whisper back.

Within the next hour though, we're all done, and the leak is finally repaired, although we're out of propane now and we need another roll of solder.

"There," Dad announces proudly. "Good as new."

"I never doubted you for a moment Dad," I lie.

I used to think that you never really stop lying to your father. You just find new reasons to do it.

So, yes, I've lied to my father a number of times over the years, but that all changed the other night. I was with him in the hospital, and wanted to find out if he was in any pain.

"How are you feeling Dad," I asked him as I stroked his head.

Without any pause, Dad breathed his response. "How do *you* feel?"

Well, what was I supposed to say?

This was typical Dad, turning things around and making it about me.

Should I lie? Should I finally tell him how I really felt about him?

Let's be honest, Dad was not an easy man to love. He could at times be bitter, sarcastic, and rarely met a grudge he couldn't hold.

But he was also loving, generous, thoughtful, and never met an act of kindness that he couldn't outdo.

How was I going to tell this man how I was going to remember him?

"How do *I* feel Dad?" I replied. "Well, it may look like I'm sad, but that's only on the outside. Inside I'm full of joy thinking about all of the happiness you brought not just to my life, but to the lives of my mother, my brothers, and my children. These aren't tears of sadness, they're tears of joy. I'm incredibly grateful."

He looked at me with eyes narrowed, almost like he didn't believe me, and then finally smiled. Maybe he figured out that I was no longer lying to him, or maybe he thought I was making another geeky reference to a movie he'd never seen. Honestly, it could go either way.

Be at peace Dad. I'll miss you.

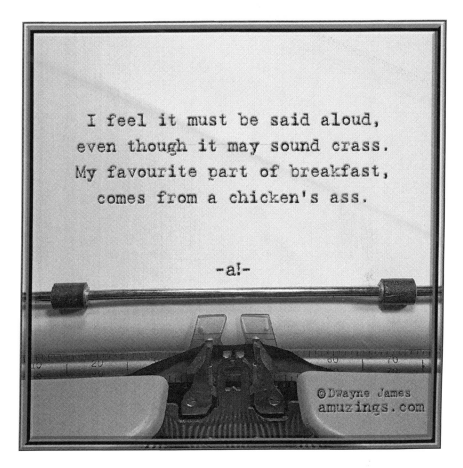

I feel it must be said aloud,
even though it may sound crass.
My favourite part of breakfast,
comes from a chicken's ass.

-a!-

©Dwayne James
amuzings.com

AND NOW, RHYMES!
Some Random Poetry... kinda

I'm not sure, but it seems to me
that she is prone to hyperbole.
Within the scope of a scant few miles,
it seems her snow fell in bigger piles.

-a!-

Whoever created the chicken,
Is giggling gleefully.
For confounding generations,
philosophically.

-a!-

Mary really had to pee,
had to pee,
had to pee.
Mary really had to pee, she really had to go.

And every where that Mary went,
Mary went,
Mary went,
Every where that Mary went, the grass refused to
grow.

Now that the boys are in daycare (at age three),
I'm thinking I should stop teaching them my
alternate versions of nursery rhymes.

-a!-

There are none quite as pretentious,
or sounding more absurd.
Than those who live in the city,
And use "cottage" as a verb.

-a!-

I learned from the best
how to be a better me,
but also from the worst
for the things I shouldn't be.

-a!-

Little boys do not play with toys,
They scatter them instead.
Yet, when they implore that they need more,
What goes thru their heads?

-a!-

The best laid plans,
it seems to me,
Can go naught but awry,
when a child needs to pee.

-a!-

Roses are red,
but when you're feeling blue,
I'll avoid you completely,
lest I catch it too.

-a!-

If your tent fits in the bag
on the very first try,
Take another look,
'cause you forgot the fly.

-a!-

Proses are read,
Kisses are blew.
I used the wrong tense,
And only you knew.

-a!-

I'm willing to admit,
that my immaturity,
makes me giggle when my wife
says, "Honeysuckle tree."

-a!-

There are many firsts in childhood,
But nothing makes the cut,
like the wonder on a boy's face,
when he first pees standing up.

-a!-

As to why my cookies taste so bad,
I'm certainly at a loss.
Could it be because vanilla looks
like Worcestershire sauce?

-a!-

If sticks and stones can break the bones
that simple words can't,
Then how can someone be 'destroyed'
by a Twitter rant?

-a!-

There is light within all darkness,
as there is darkness in all light.
Like a shadow in the sunshine,
Or a candle in the night.

-a!-

When I talk to both the twins at once,
I call them 'W'.
I tell them, "It's, of course, because,
there are two of 'U'."

-a!-

This condiment is half the fat,
That's what the label says.
So now I'm eating twice as much,
from my jar of mayonnaise.

-a!-

Ode to breakfast:
Of all the wonders this world can boast,
Naught compares to honey on toast.

-a!-

"Thou art beautiful, as like a rose,
exactly as thouest art,
Unless thou exposeth too much thong
at the village Wal-Mart."
- Shakespeare

-a!-

God said of the dove:
"Peace will he symbolize,
but just to keep him humble,
he shall squeak when he flies."

-a!-

We see with more than just our Eyes,
We feel with more than just our Hearts.
The limit is more than just the Skies,
The sum is more than all its Parts.

-a!-

Here I stand, about to cry.
Came into this room, and don't know why.

-a!-

It's always made me wonder,
and now it makes me laugh:
If my underwear's
part of a pair,
where is the other half?

-a!-

THE MOMENT

There's a moment between waking and dreaming,
when the morning's still one with the night.
When your dreams slowly form into feelings,
and that's when she let in the light.

So quickly I pulled up my pillow,
to cover my head and my eyes.
She said "Listen to that. Can you hear it?"
and looked through the window outside.

At first, I heard nothing but silence,
and as the moments bled slowly away
I could hear birds singing to sunrise,
and somewhere a loon's lonely wail.

I noticed she smiled very loudly,
and she asked "Do you know what this means?"
"No, not exactly," I answered.
"But when can I go back to sleep?"

She stepped out of our tent as she answered,
and dove silently into the lake.
"There's a moment between waking and dreaming,
and you're not exactly awake."

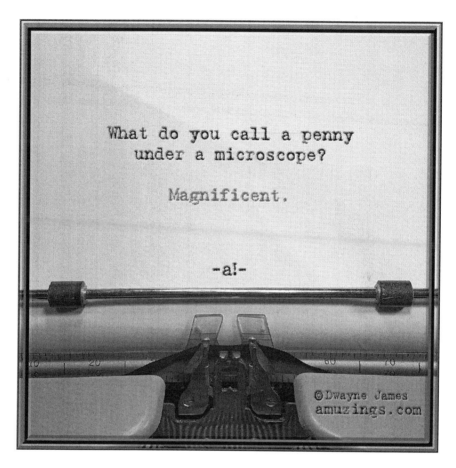

What do you call a penny
under a microscope?

Magnificent.

-a!-

©Dwayne James
amuzings.com

CHILDISH HUMOUR
Jokes specifically by and/or for children

My six-year old made a joke this morning:

Him: Knock knock.

Me: Who's there?

Him: Interrupting pig.

Me: Interrupting pig who?

. . .

Him: What sound does a pig make again?

-a!-

According to my sons, "policy" means to act like
a police officer, as in "the person in the
uniform was acting all 'policy' and stuff."

-a!-

Not having the Google Map app sing, "I'm the
map, I'm the map, I'm the map..." when it
launches seems like a wasted opportunity to me.

-a!-

How did the trees feel in Spring when their
foliage returned?

Re-leaved.

-a!-

How do sheep say "Merry Christmas"?

Fleece Navidad.

-a!-

What did one unleavened bread product say to
another loaf who was being hysterical?

Don't bannock.

-a!-

A problem only a child would understand: "PHEW!
It took me forEVER to colour that sky!"

-a!-

How do cows make a choice?

Eenie meanie mienie mooooooo.

-a!-

How many women who are symbolically married to
the Church does it take to screw in a light
bulb?

Nun.

That's odd. That was a whole lot funnier in my
dream last night.

-a!-

What fees do oranges and bananas pay to attend
University?

Fruition.

-a!-

What did air say to water when they had been re-
introduced after a long separation?

I mist you.

-a!-

What do you call a form you have to sign?

Something you oughta-graph.

-a!-

Why don't the French count to ten?

They get to nine and they've had a neuf.

-a!-

My joke for the boys as I helped get them
dressed this morning:

Personally, I call them "underthere" because I
know where they are.

-a!-

What do cows wear under their clothes?

Udderwear.

-a!-

What do you call a farm animal that likes to give directions?

A chicken-guy-ding.

-a!-

How did the tomato and mushroom soups complete their marriage ceremony?

They consomméd it.

-a!-

What musical instrument is the most agreeable?

The accordion.

-a!-

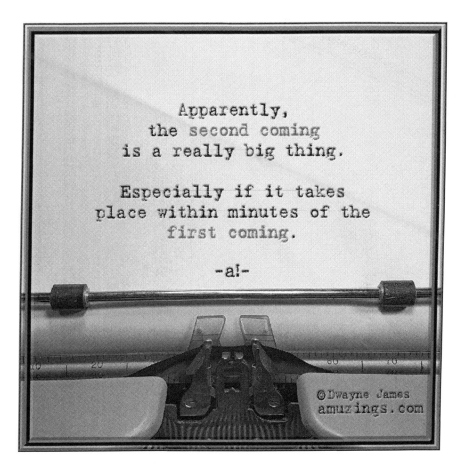

Apparently,
the second coming
is a really big thing.

Especially if it takes
place within minutes of the
first coming.

-a!-

©Dwayne James
amuzings.com

IMMATURE HUMOUR
Jokes specifically for adults who still act like children

Little known fact: Mary didn't actually carry
Jesus to term.

It was a *premature immaculation*.

-a!-

Sexually dominant math teachers always want to
be the numerator.

-a!-

If an apology comes from the heart, where does
an analogy come from?

-a!-

"Did I peak in high school?" he answered.
"Several times. Occasionally even with a
partner."

-a!-

If children's literature has taught me anything,
it's that old ladies don't have a gag reflex.

-a!-

Quite frankly, I'm amazed how the solution to
most problems is simply more lubrication.

-a!-

As everyone stares into their pinprick cameras
to watch the eclipse, I'm over here saying, "See!
Tiny pricks are good for something!"

-a!-

So, apparently last night, a TV reporter
fractured a fibula while covering a story.

It was leg-breaking news.

-a!-

I love my Dyson vacuum as much as any man can
love an inanimate object that... um, sucks really
well.

My customer testimonial needs work.

-a!-

I misheard something while we were eating
pancakes the other day, and it's got me thinking
that milk could actually be called "nipple
syrup".

-a!-

I could be wrong, but I'm pretty sure that I'm
now going steady with the young woman who
adjusted my seatbelt on the last ride at the
amusement park.

-a!-

Say what you want about abstinence, but until
you put "a penis" in it, "happiness" is just the
sound effect "phs".

-a!-

It's all about context. For example, you can say
that a radio station "has the greatest hits",
but you probably shouldn't say the same thing
about your waitress.

-a!-

BUBER:
a ride-sharing service for women with large...
y'know what? I'm not even gonna finish that
thought.

-a!-

If you lose weight through sexual activity,
you're burning cal "O" ries.

-a!-

A toot suite: an ordered set of orchestral
instrumentals composed entirely from the sounds
of flatulence.

-a!-

I've always been disappointed that, when asked to "Select Sex" on an online form, the drop-down menu never offers "infrequent" as an option.

-a!-

Oh NOW I remember what the string on my hand is for.

My fingers were engaging in a little light bondage yesterday.

-a!-

How many paraphilias does it take to screw a light bulb?

-a!-

When someone says, "bare with me," I naturally assume that it's an invitation to get naked.

-a!-

Is it just me, or does the phrase "comes in like a lion and goes out like a lamb" sound like the description of something in the Kama Sutra?

-a!-

The other day, I made a gargling noise by mistake when I was yawning.

"Hey, I just did Chewbacca!" I announced, pretty damned pleased with myself.

"What?" asked my driving companion, sensing perhaps that I was about to be inappropriate.

"You're right," I conceded. "Look at him. You don't do Chewie; Chewie does you."

-a!-

Innuendo marries a tongue twister:

That's what she said selling seashells by the
seashore.

-a!-

As much as I'd like to clone myself so that I
could get more done during the day, I'd only get
hopelessly distracted by my own rugged
handsomeness.

I mean really, how does my wife do it?

-a!-

It occurs to me that, when the right hand
doesn't know what the left one is doing,
masturbation is that much more interesting.

-a!-

Whenever I ask my wife what she wants to do
tonight, I'm always secretly thinking to myself,
"Please say *me*, please say *me*..."

-a!-

What do you call a man who is too quick to offer
short, exclamatory, speech utterances?

A premature ejaculator!

-a!-

How do you get helium to reproduce?

Introduce him to some *shelium*.

-a!-

"Did you pass gas?" she asked.

"Actually," I replied. "I didn't just pass it, I'm pretty sure I aced it."

-a!-

It is beyond me that, in this day and age, we have yet to invent a toilet bowl that suppresses sound rather than enhancing it.

-a!-

Why is it called 'Black Friday'?

Because 'Good Luck Finding a Fucking Parking Spot Today' makes a lousy acronym.

-a!-

Q-tips feel soooooo good when you put them in your ear. That's why I call them "ear dildos."

-a!-

Brand messaging suggests that if something sounds like a JOB, nobody will want to do it.

On that note, may I humbly recommend that we start calling them "blow-parties" and "hand-celebrations"?

-a!-

It's better to be a little behind than a huge ass.

-a!-

Friction is grossly underappreciated. Think about it. Without friction none of us would even be here.

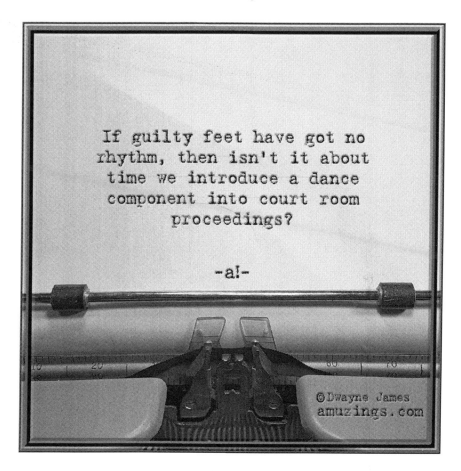

QnoA
Questions I've posed with no Answers?

What if the change I want to see in the world is invisible?

What then smart guy?

-a!-

I just opened up a pomegranate and took the seeds out.

Is the kitchen supposed to look like a crime scene now?

-a!-

Do gay chefs come out of the pantry instead of
the closet?

-a!-

Without punctuation, does a sentence ever
really end

-a!-

After two clowns have an argument, do they have
makeup sex?

-a!-

Shouldn't the diet version of "Thousand Islands"
salad dressing be called "Nine Hundred Islands"?

-a!-

If an animated GIF is on repeat in a browser tab
that nobody is watching, is it still playing?

-a!-

If an animated GIF is on repeat in a browser tab
that nobody is watching, will people still
mispronounce it?

-a!-

Do people sneeze in the same accent in which
they speak?

-a!-

If your motto is "Everything in moderation,"
shouldn't you only practice it some of the time?

-a!-

If people started to recognize the Sabbath on Friday, could they start saying "Thank Friday, it's God"?

-a!-

Did you ever notice that "I'm voting" is a perfect anagram for "vomiting."

Kinda sums up 2016 doesn't it? #USElection

-a!-

If pixies are covered in magic dust that can be used to make people fly, then why do the pixies themselves have wings?

-a!-

Does time ever get paranoid that so many people are trying to kill it?

-a!-

Is there a law against the use of an air horn beside a person illegally smoking within nine meters of a public entrance?

Asking for a friend.

-a!-

I think the battery in my battery tester might be dying, but how do I find out?

-a!-

Is the active version of the word "vacation" to "vacate"?

-a!-

Is cursive writing the best way to swear in
text?

-a!-

When lingerie companies lay people off, do they
give out pink slips?

-a!-

Most shoelaces have a tough, nigh-unbreakable
core.

Which begs the question: why isn't the whole
damn shoelace made from the same material?

-a!-

When a grape has an identity crisis, does it
lose its "raisin d'être"?

-a!-

Isn't eating maple syrup a little too much like
drinking tree blood?

-a!-

If you're having enough fun to make time fly at
88 miles per hour, will time start to go
backwards?

-a!-

Are people who write "open letters" unable to
buy a stamp?

Maybe we should take up a collection for them or
something.

-a!-

Shouldn't know-it-alls already know how
obnoxious they are?

-a!-

What are sleeping dogs lying about?
Being asleep?

-a!-

Isn't "Presented without comment" in itself a
comment?

-a!-

Do soldiers for hire do it in the mercenary
position?

-a!-

Why aren't antique canoes called caolds?

-a!-

Isn't it a little bit coincidental that the word
"lingerie" has the word "linger" within it?

-a!-

If light travels faster than sound, then why is
it that our hearing is often the first to go?

-a!-

Is Daylight being threatened somehow?
Then why is there an annual effort to save it?

-a!-

Shouldn't the opposite of forgiveness be
aftgiveness?

-a!-

If you're late for something, do you arrive
"just out time?"

-a!-

If we named new-borns the same way that toddlers
named their stuffies, would everyone be named
"baby"?

-a!-

Do you think it's possible that it was a tow-
truck driver that coined the phrase: "There are
no accidents, only opportunities"?

-a!-

Does GMC stand for "Genetically Modified Car"?

-a!-

If I told the makers of my phone that I liked
the sound that it makes when calls come in,
would I be giving the phone a ringing
endorsement?

-a!-

Is baby spinach the veal of the vegetable world?

-a!-

If the saying "nothing good ever lasts" is such good advice, then why's it still around after all these years?

-a!-

Do the bees who make hard honey need more fibre in their diets?

-a!-

Is a "beeline" an optional route?

Wouldn't it be better to "make an a-line" for something? A "Beeline" sounds like something you'd do if the "a-line" didn't work out.

-a!-

"Have a good weekend if I don't see you," she said.

"What if I *do* see her?" I wondered. "Can I still have a good weekend?"

-a!-

Hey, can workers in a cigarette factory smoke in the workplace?

-a!-

If a person were really bad at understanding percentages, would they know that they were failing math?

-a!-

Personally, I've always wondered what would happen if I yelled, "Theater!" in a crowded fire.

-a!-

If a person were to be taken over by an evil
spirit for a second time, has that person been
repossessed?

-a!-

According to the Dalai Lama, perception shapes
our reality.

By that logic then, if you lost track of time,
would you still continue to age?

-a!-

Y'know, I've always wondered: Just why is Scott
so great anyhow?

-a!-

Shouldn't rare earth magnets be harder to
acquire?

I mean, you can buy them pretty much everywhere.

-a!-

If a minister makes a silly joke about something
serious, is that person being irreverend?

-a!-

Has it occurred to anyone that "x" doesn't want
to be found?

-a!-

It's 2015. We have a gender-equal cabinet yet,
inexplicably, commemorative poppies still don't
come with a complimentary Band-Aid.

-a!-

If Peter Mansbridge explains something to you, would it be called "mansbridgesplaining?"

-a!-

All this time, and nobody has ever mistaken the TARDIS for a port-a-potty?

-a!-

Did Bruce or Ashton ever refer to their wife Demi as the better half?

-a!-

I've always wondered: was there actually a time when rat's asses *were* given?

-a!-

Shouldn't the past tense of "telephone" be "toldephone"?

-a!-

Why are there more than ten X-Men?

-a!-

Why do some people have a manicure every few weeks?

Isn't a cure supposed to be permanent?

-a!-

Flies are biting me. I forget, does that indicate an impeding storm, or that that the anti-Christ is coming?

-a!-

Shouldn't the spirit wear for Catholic schools
be called "Holy Spirit Wear?"

-a!-

Do you think parents of serial killers ever
encouraged their kids with the phrase: "Go knock
'em dead honey" ?

-a!-

Are snap peas quick to judge?

-a!-

How long does one have to stand under the
Supermoon for their super powers to develop?

Asking for a friend.

-a!-

If you're not completely altruistic, but you
mean well, are you partruistic?

-a!-

If ever Elon Musk is involved in a protracted
scandal, will it be called "Elon-gate?"

-a!-

I just read that we all have that one friend who
says stupid, embarrassing things, but none of my
friends do that.

Wait. It's me isn't it?

-a!-

Is "thesaurus" another word for a dinosaur?

-a!-

If "hubris" is an extreme arrogance or pride in
oneself, then why isn't it called "mebris"?

-a!-

Why don't the fruit flies that have infested my
kitchen build their own home?

There are plenty of dried up Rice Krispies that
could be used as construction material.

-a!-

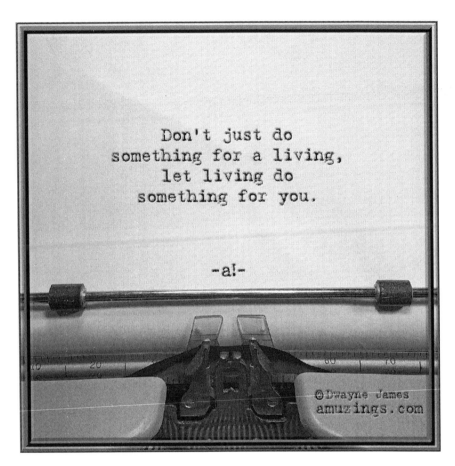

Don't just do
something for a living,
let living do
something for you.

-a!-

©Dwayne James
amuzings.com

GINGER SOUP FOR THE SOUL
Inspirational, often with a twist

When it comes to self-improvement, I'm pretty
laidback knowing that good things come to those
who wait.

That's why I'm not seeking to find myself. I'll
just wait for myself to find me.

-a!-

Instead of belittling someone, why not try
bebigging them instead?

-a!-

Rescue workers prove beyond a shadow of a doubt
that it's not fools who rush in.

-a!-

If life is but a dream, I'd much rather be lucid
than "woke."

-a!-

It's better to be nice to people in the future
rather than fixated on what they did in the
past.

Yes, it's better to be kind than to rewind.

-a!-

In my dream last night, Robin Williams was my
doctor.

"I'm not dead," he told me. "I'm hanging out in
hospitals making people feel better."

-a!-

You don't make a living creating art, you live
your making.

-a!-

I find the phrase "anything is possible" far too
limiting. Personally, I prefer to believe that
anything is probable.

-a!-

I'm not just living the dream, I'm dreaming the
life!

-a!-

Love doesn't conquer hate; not everything is a
battle.

Love simply absorbs hate, and turns it into a
warm breeze.

-a!-

My vibes say not to trust much of this "New Age"
advice, but it's the same "New Age" advice that
tells me to trust my vibes, so I'm torn.

-a!-

Love. It's the gift that keeps on living.

-a!-

I think I'll name a future painting "Happiness,"
and then tell people that they can buy it.

-a!-

"That is how you limit yourself," said the wise
old woman. "By thinking that only some things
are meant to be when it is *everything* that is
meant to be."

-a!-

It has come to my attention that, occasionally,
wishes would like to be something other than
horses.

-a!-

Apparently, after studying mindfulness, Popeye
has changed his slogan to ,"I yam *where* I yam."

-a!-

Without its paradoxes, the universe would be full of contradictions.

-a!-

Starting the day feeling grateful. Seems like a "grate" way to start any day!

Thanks!

-a!-

I've discovered that Heaven and Earth are a lot lighter when you get friends and family to help you move them.

-a!-

I'm not so much interested anymore in divining the meaning of life, as I am in pursuing a life of meaning.

-a!-

"Follow me," she said. "Just mind the fullness."

-a!-

They may not have handles, but grudges are remarkably easy to hold.

-a!-

Sometimes, the best way to find your way out of a dark place when you can't find a light, is simply to feel your way.

-a!-

It's simple really: the way we see the world is
the way the world is seen.

-a!-

Naturally, the question I'm more interested in
is: "Does magic believe in me?"

-a!-

When opportunity knocks, make sure it isn't just
trying to sneak into your house to scope out
your furnace.

It's sneaky like that.

-a!-

The truth is irrelevant when you're motivated to
believe a lie.

-a!-

The real experts - the ones who make something
look both fun and easy - will be the first to
tell you that it is.

-a!-

It's not the pen that's mightier than the SWORD,
but the WORDS that the pen creates.

It's no coincidence that the two are a perfect
anagram.

-a!-

When you're moved by forces that nobody else can
see, you've just experienced the wind in the
candle.

-a!-

Self-effacing literally means to erase yourself.

Where humility is definitely important, a pencil
that erases itself doesn't leave much of a mark.

-a!-

For those of you who need an extra day between
Saturday and Sunday, just try to look at it
differently: there are five whole days between
Sunday and Saturday.

-a!-

Why do I smile in the face of uncertainty?

Because, it's still better than the alternative.

-a!-

May you live past the point of no regret.

-a!-

Some speak of daring to dream as if it's a risk,
when it's daring NOT to dream that is far more
dangerous.

-a!-

Personally, I prefer to see it from the
perspective that we're only as weak as the
strongest link.

-a!-

I'm pretty sure that, of all life's afflictions,
bitterness will kill you faster than anything
this side of a speeding bus.

-a!-

As much as I would like to count my blessings, I
fear the numbering system as we know it is
woefully inadequate.

-a!-

Personally, I prefer the expression "Too good
NOT to be true."

-a!-

To say that seeing an act of kindness restores
my faith in humanity implies that I'd lost it in
the first place.

The good will ALWAYS outweigh the bad, it just
doesn't make for interesting TV.

-a!-

Things may not always go as planned, but they
usually go as expected.

-a!-

The thing about pissing matches is that, even if
you win, there's a pretty good chance that
you're still covered in urine.

-a!-

If the alternative to not fitting in anywhere is
floating free everywhere, then suddenly it
doesn't seem so bad.

-a!-

Life is frequently paradoxical. You'll know what
I mean the next time you press a button labelled
"ON" in order to turn something OFF.

-a!-

"Everything's a balance," said the wise old woman. "You can do anything you put your mind to, but only if your heart's in it."

-a!-

I've often wondered if Karma takes offense when it gets called a bitch, because if there's one person you DO NOT want to piss off, it's Karma.

-a!-

She had a beautiful simile.

Like an upside-down rainbow wrapped in cotton candy clouds.

-a!-

Such is the paradoxical nature of dreams that they always come true, even when they don't.

-a!-

I am certainly no longer the boy I used to be.

But that's OK, because I've become the man I never was.

-a!-

My new motto:

Don't just do something for a living, let living do something for you.

-a!-

Anyone who's ever used a magnifying glass knows, if you focus on any one thing for too long, you're likely to start a fire.

-a!-

The shortest distance between two points is a
straight line.

Unless space is curved.

Then, the shortest distance is your imagination.

-a!-

Do you know the real reason "slow and steady"
wins the race?

"Slow and steady" doesn't care that there's a
race.

-a!-

When I got to the mountain top, I asked the wise
woman, "Why do children ask so many questions?"
and she just laughed and laughed.

-a!-

I'm no psychologist, but it occurs to me that
the only thing wrong with some people is that
they think that something is wrong with them.

-a!-

Sometimes, dreams come true and, other times,
truths become dreams.

-a!-

It's all about perspective.

For example, if you use the 24-hour clock, then
being in the 11th hour isn't nearly as dire.

-a!-

Best advice I've ever given my children:

Apologizing is easy. Holding a grudge? Now that takes some work.

-a!-

Life is like a game of Jeopardy. The answer is actually a question.

-a!-

I have to admit that death doesn't really scare me that much.

Life, on the other hand, frequently frightens the royal piss out of me.

-a!-

After a while, all the words of wisdom sound the same.

-a!-

While impressive to hear of those who can remain lucid and awake while dreaming, I've always been more amazed with those who can do it when they're already awake.

-a!-

I don't necessarily believe that life is unfair.

However, I am absolutely convinced that it's ironic.

-a!-

The fear of being contaminated by an unfamiliar idea is like being afraid that taking a drink of water will turn you into a fish.

-a!-

I've been around long enough now to realize
that, the more things change, the more I'm
reminded that I can no longer remember what they
used to be like in the first place.

-a!-

I've never liked the term "random act of
kindness" because it sounds like it happened by
mistake. Personally, I prefer "premeditated act
of kindness."

-a!-

My New Year's Resolution from January of 2018:

This year, I'm going to keep my opinion to
myself and stop telling people what to do, and I
think you should do the same too.

-a!-

Serenity:

It's not about finding a peaceful moment to
think, it's thinking that every moment is
peaceful.

-a!-

SHARING is DIVINE

But so is having the whole bowl of popcorn to
yourself.

-a!-

People who live in glass houses, should never go
naked.

-a!-

With all this talk about fighting FIRE with
FIRE, has anybody considered using WATER?

-a!-

Work hard to give your kids a future, but play
hard to give them a present too.

-a!-

Deterministic destiny is the unerring belief
that you are exactly where you are supposed to
be, and doing exactly what it is that you are
meant to be doing, simply because you are
exactly where you are, and doing exactly what it
is that you are doing.

-a!-

For many creative thinkers, the goal is to think
outside the box. Most of the time, this is
perfectly fine, but problems occur when we
forget that it is the box that gives our ideas
context, as well as shared meaning. Think too
far outside of it, and other people won't know
what the hell you're talking about.

That's a tip kids, now *bird* with it.

See what I mean?

-a!-

INSPIRATIONAL MESSAGES WITH CAVEATS:

"Just listen to your heart, unless it is telling you to hurt or kill people."

-a!-

"Be the change you want to see in the world, unless what you want to see is lots of naked people."

-a!-

"Follow your dream, unless your dream is to rob a convenience store."

-a!-

"Do what lights you up, unless what lights you up is setting fire to buildings."

-a!-

GINGER SNAPS
A propos of nothing much...

Apparently, in palliative care units, obese women are told not to sing in front of the terminally ill patients.

-a!-

The part of a song that grabs everyone's attention should be called the "vocal point."

You're welcome.

-a!-

I smacked a fly so hard earlier that I discovered a number of sub-atomic particles as a result.

-a!-

It's ironic that ducks have such long necks, because this makes it harder for them to lower their heads quickly.

-a!-

Today, I discovered that, if you put the saw blade on backwards, it does NOT put the wood back together as I'd previously assumed.

-a!-

Ever notice that "He's a moron" is an almost perfect anagram for "Hormones"?

Kinda explains teenaged boys doesn't it?

-a!-

Apparently, during the American Civil War, the North created the idea of Santa's sled as a way to demoralize the South by making them think that they would miss out on Xmas because they didn't have enough snow for the sled to slide on.

They were literally *Rebels without a Claus.*

-a!-

I just changed the title on my LinkedIn profile for technical communications to: "Message Therapist."

I can't wait to see what kind of searches I appear in now!

-a!-

If you're going to have a lot of balls in the
air, put helium in them first.

-a!-

Disappointed to discover that, after years of
studying history so as not to be condemned to
repeat it, they were grading on a curve.

-a!-

Click-baiting from 1928: "He takes a loaf of
bread and a bunch of knives and you won't
believe what he does with them all."

-a!-

The time of night when I'm heading to bed is
when my neighbours wonder if I'm sending Morse
code messages when I've just mixed up the light
switches again.

-a!-

The maple syrup on my breakfast plate just
touched my sausage.

I am *this* close to calling 911.

-a!-

Isn't it funny that, when people tell you how
they avoided a phishing scam, they make it sound
much bigger than it actually was?

-a!-

I never say, "Bye now" because I'm too much of a
procrastinator.

-a!-

I'm probably not the first to say this but,
before the internet came along, I used to think
my ideas were a lot more original.

-a!-

Sometimes, it's a daily struggle to keep the
proper balance of leftovers in the fridge so as
not to overwhelm the Tupperware drawer.

-a!-

As a person, I feel I've grown beyond "one-
upmanship".

It's now "one-uppersonship" thank-you-very-much.

-a!-

I just took an internet quiz to measure how
mysterious I am, but it won't give me the
results.

Well played internet quiz. Well played indeed.

-a!-

The grocery store cashier just asked me if the
apples in my cart were delicious.

"I dunno," I replied. "I haven't tasted them
yet."

-a!-

There are two types of people in this world.
Those who can play the "Can Can" on a musical
instrument, and those who saw this joke coming
from a mile away.

-a!-

I'm pretty sure I just heard a woman claim to be so poor that she didn't "have two nipples to rub together."

Well, I'm off to the holodeck...

-a!-

I'll never understand why Royal parade routes go in a single direction when the Queen can move in any direction.

-a!-

I'm done rushing around. From now on, I'm walking errands.

-a!-

I can only assume that butterflies, being born as glorified worms, are forever in a state of shock and constantly wondering, "Seriously, what the fuck happened to me?"

-a!-

An online survey is asking what I would most like to see in a cookie.

Hmmmm. I don't see an option for "My teeth".

-a!-

Verily, thou hast not properly emptied the dishwasher unless thou hast slopped water from a seemingly empty vessel onto the floor.

-a!-

My new year's resolution is the same as last year's: 1600 x 900.

-a!-

What you refer to as my tenuous grasp on reality
is what I call my vivid imagination.

-a!-

I always like to use the self-check-out because
I always like to check myself out.

-a!-

If only I had an easy way to count all of the
calculators that I've lost or misplaced over the
years...

-a!-

Idea for the title of a new soap opera for the
social media generation: *"One Like to Give."*

-a!-

When you take a sharp intake of breath in order
to expel the mosquito you just swallowed, and
you swallow two more.

Eww.

-a!-

People who love musical theater are some of the
smartest people I know.

Every single one of them knows how many minutes
there are in a year.

-a!-

I'll see your round hole and raise you a square
peg.

-a!-

I don't know what's louder, the sound of the
chainsaw, or me yelling, "Now I am a man!"
whenever I use it.

-a!-

If anyone wants me, I'll be in that big open
field, flitting about randomly, trying to get a
human murmuration going.

-a!-

Facebook just asked me "What's going on,
Dwayne?"

If I were more like Norm Peterson, I'd reply,
"Right now, I'd rather talk about what's
going *in* Dwayne!"

Cue the canned laughter.

-a!-

You know what Bare Naked Ladies?

You're right. I HAVE always wanted a monkey.

-a!-

They say dress for the job you want.

So what does it say that I'm going to a job
interview wearing a suit I bought for a funeral?

-a!-

Decided to shake up the cliché this morning, and
put BOTH pant legs on at the same time!

Funny, it doesn't feel any different yet.

-a!-

I don't want to brag, but I just used the
washroom and didn't take my phone.

-a!-

People who are always walking on egg shells
should probably sweep more often.

-a!-

I'm told that people will believe pretty much
anything that they're told.

-a!-

The internet these days is so narcissistic.

Lately, it's all about meme.

-a!-

I like to keep the house cold overnight so that
if I forget to put something back in the fridge
before I go to bed, it doesn't go bad.

-a!-

So apparently, I'm a brown-noser & a suck-up.

But my friends already knew this, because I've
always said how clever and perceptive they are.

-a!-

Trying to shed weight?

The fastest way to feel like you're swimming in
your clothes is to jump in a lake fully-dressed.

-a!-

I will now answer only to the title "Lord of the Pith."

-a!-

The weather called.

It's tired of trying to live up to our expectations, so from now on, it's doing whatever the hell it wants.

-a!-

Oh, that explains why I was so empty-headed last week when I was sick.

I was using the Vick's VAPID rub.

-a!-

When I reach for the light switch and miss, I like to swat uselessly four or five more times just to make absolutely sure that I've missed it.

-a!-

So, apparently we're drinking trace amounts of prescription drugs that get into our drinking water through our collective urine.

Wait. What?

We're drinking urine?

-a!-

If I could fill out a survey about last night's sleep I'd have to say that it was 10 for excellent, and that I would definitely recommend it to friends.

-a!-

How about we select the next Pope by way of a
reality show called "The Amazing Grace".

-a!-

"Thank you for the Thank You card," I said.

"Thank you for thanking me for the Thank you
card," she replied.

Sometimes, it's exhausting being Canadian.

-a!-

According to my son's Father's Day card, my best
attribute is my ability to pick things up.

Truly, I couldn't do it without him.

-a!-

Since hindsight is 20/20, I'm going to start
walking backwards.

-a!-

The hills are alive with the sound of Daddy
finding the hole in the oven mitts.

-a!-

I don't always have to have the last word in an
argument, but I do like to have the last
punctuation mark.

Period.

-a!-

Never trust a cow when it comes to weather.

When it gets bad, they lie.

-a!-

Webinar presentation tip:

During a live streaming demonstration, don't
type the word "analysis" if you're going to
pause indefinitely four letters in to make sure
that you're spelling it right.

-a!-

Of course I use a shampoo to control dry scalp.
It's called "skin cream".

-a!-

All this time, I thought assassination was a
country with a LOT of donkeys.

-a!-

I have a strict policy against making passive
aggressive posts, unlike others who shall remain
nameless.

-a!-

Today, one of my co-workers was telling us that
she wasn't very good in the high-school band
because she sucked at playing the trumpet.

"There's your first problem," I offered. "You're
supposed to blow."

-a!-

I'm guessing that this website form that is
asking me "What is 1+1?" isn't going to accept
"a mathematical equation" as an answer.

-a!-

It's all fun and games until somebody plays "The Macarena".

-a!-

Yardwork used to be the kind of thing that only ever happened to somebody else.

-a!-

There are three kinds of people in this world:

Those who can do math, and those who know where this joke is going...

-a!-

My definition of a fine dining establishment: one where you have to ASK for the ketchup.

-a!-

Not only has that ship sailed, it exploded and sunk on its maiden voyage.

Then they made it into a movie that crashed and burned at the box office.

-a!-

If I knew then what I know now, I'd probably get arrested for insider trading.

-a!-

My generation is more creative because our pirated movies were scrambled, and we had to use our imaginations to figure out what was going on.

-a!-

Am I self-serving? Before I answer that, I have
to ask: what's in it for me?

-a!-

There is a certain kind of joy that can only
come from your car when, in the presence of the
mechanic, it actually makes the noise it always
does.

-a!-

Sometimes, if the things on my "TO-DO" list are
especially dramatic, I call it my "TA-DAH" list.

-a!-

Those who admire themselves in a mirror while
standing in line are waiting in vain.

-a!-

Whenever I melt butter and cream together, I
imagine that the butter is yelling at me: "Make
up your damned mind!"

-a!-

When someone says, "May all your dreams come
true," I say, "I hope not. I really don't want
to go to high school naked. Again."

-a!-

As I've aged, I've discovered that socks are
like toilet paper: the thicker, the better.

-a!-

Never say to a sick person in an adjustable
hospital bed, "It's time to put you down."

-a!-

So, apparently volume shampoo is NOT intended
for those who are hard of hearing.

Who knew?

-a!-

Whenever I see a crosswalk, I like to smile and
say something nice to it in order to lift its
spirits.

-a!-

Apparently, Gal Gadot's first name used to be
"Gail" but, as a child, she played with an
Official Red Ryder Carbine-Action Two-Hundred-
Shot Range Model Air Rifle.

-a!-

Believe it or not, the original Semitic alphabet
had two letter I's until, one Xmas, it was given
an Official Red Ryder Carbine-Action Two-
Hundred-Shot Range Model Air Rifle.

-a!-

One day, the alphabet didn't listen to its
parents and was running with scissors. This is
what happened:

ABCDEFGHJKLMNOPQRSTUVWXYZ.

-a!-

At first, the "yes" side appeared to have won by
a single vote, until that vote was taken away in
a verbal recount.

I guess it's true that it's all fun and games
until somebody loses an "aye."

-a!-

Change doesn't scare me, but paper money does.
Especially tens.

I don't know why.

-a!-

The journey of a thousand miles starts with the
packing of your toothbrush.

-a!-

I asked the man at the bar why he was so sad.

"My psychic just told me that there was no point
in me booking another appointment," he said.

-a!-

Earlier, I put my smartphone down beside the
smartTV, and the two of them immediately started
arguing over who was more intelligent.

-a!-

Woohoo!

I'm having one of those "I found a matching
Tupperware lid on the first try" kinda days.

-a!-

I dropped a vitamin on the floor and couldn't
find it, so I dropped another one to show me
what I was looking for.

Now I can't find either one.

-a!-

I dunno about you, but I always thought of the phrase, "You can't make this up" as a challenge.

-a!-

The problem with today's world is that far too many opinions start with the phrase, "the problem with today's world."

-a!-

Apparently, this new house has three potential sources of water.

Well, well, well.

-a!-

I've always wondered, since it's served cold, is gazpacho soup revenge for something?

-a!-

Actually, according to most cookbooks, revenge is a dish best served either passive-aggressively or sarcastically.

-a!-

My watch isn't five minutes slow; it's 23 hours and 55 minutes fast.

-a!-

Some days are prolific, and others, it's all I can do to finish my

-a!-

I'd settle for just teaching the world to hum the same tune for a while.

-a!-

Most of the time, an imagination is a wonderful
thing.

Less so when it's three in the morning, and
you've just heard a noise you can't identify.

Especially when you're camping.

-a!-

Imagine my surprise when I finally visited the
Middle East to find that the shepherds there
don't wear housecoats while watching their
flocks by night.

Apparently, the grade school Christmas pageants
of my youth were slightly less than accurate.

-a!-

Perhaps ironically, William of Ockham had a full
beard.

Look it up.

-a!-

One is the loneliest number.

Unless you're a Buddhist.

-a!-

I know that I, for one, wouldn't be at all sad
if humans lacked emotions.

-a!-

My apologies. Upon closer inspection, it appears
that they *were* my monkeys after all.

-a!-

Got home today to find that the house had been
taken over by fruit flies.

Not sure how they acquired the deed, but we've
got a week to pack.

-a!-

Perhaps ironically, starting your post with "I
bet you won't read this post" pretty much
guarantees it.

-a!-

If you've seen one animal that is the last of
its species, you've seen them all.

Literally.

-a!-

Wanna hear something magical?

I have a machine in the basement that makes
water out of thin air!

Thin air, I tell ya! It's unreal.

-a!-

I have headphones that weren't working right
until I put them through the wash by mistake.

Now they're perfect.

Gonna wash my old laptop next.

-a!-

A man who can toot his own horn is very
flexible.

-a!-

The problem with being eccentric is that people think you're weird.

The nice thing about being eccentric, is that you just don't care.

-a!-

The canoe keeps coming loose at the dock.

Now, either I've forgotten how to tie a knot, or the ducks are having some fun with me.

-a!-

Her tone of voice seemed to imply: If I sound arrogant, it's just because you're too stupid to understand what I'm actually saying.

-a!-

You can get facial tissues infused with skin cream, yet not Irish cream.

Seems like a missed opportunity to me.

-a!-

I just bought grapes.

Now taking bets as to which ones will be eaten, and which ones will be ignored on the bottom of the bowl until they grow mold.

-a!-

And the most important lesson I've learned by having friends and family who are police officers is never to mention that fact when I've been pulled over by a police officer.

-a!-

Man. I slept so well last night there was
sawdust on the pillow when I woke up this
morning.

-a!-

If you can't say something nice, then at least
be witty about it so that people don't realize
it's an insult.

-a!-

Who's got two thumbs and doesn't like to point
fingers?

This guy!

Oh, wait...

-a!-

The hottest new emoticon is a white cow in a
snowstorm.

Behold:

-a!-

Fart jokes are kinda like farts themselves.

They're funnier when you make them.

-a!-

It's not so much that spoons and coffee mugs go
to die in my workshop, but it is apparently
where they like to hide out.

-a!-

Did you know that a cat is nine times more
likely to get depressed in middle age in
thinking that it's done nothing with its lives?

-a!-

"Your pretty stupid if you don't know the
difference between there, their and they're,"
she wrote without a hint of irony.

-a!-

Apparently the answer to who I was in a former
life is: "younger me with more hair."

-a!-

The defoliated tree in my backyard just confided
in me by saying, "I didn't downsize my
workforce, I initiated a resource action."

-a!-

I consider all inquiries pertaining to the
current time to be "gotcha" questions.

-a!-

And now, under the category of less is more:

-a!-

I'm discovering that writing is less about
finding the perfect synonym, and more about
finding the perfect segue.

On that note...

-a!-

WHEN NO NORMAL TOAST WILL DO:

Let us all raise our glasses this morning for my
favourite toast:

To the Batmobile!

-a!-

And my second favourite toast:

To infinity... and beyond!

-a!-

My third favourite toast:

To the top of the porch, to the top of the wall!

-a!-

And lest we forget the honourable mention:

To have and to hold!

-a!-

PHILOSOPHICAL MUSINGS

I may not really exist.

At least according to the automatic soap
dispenser in the men's room.

-a!-

I'm having both chicken and eggs for lunch.

Purely from a philosophical stand point, I'm
unsure which to eat first.

-a!-

Philosophically speaking, the phrase "there are
no original ideas" should not exist because the
first time it was said, it was technically an
original idea, and it should have cancelled
itself out.

-a!-

It turns out that there actually *is* a reason
behind it all.

Unfortunately that reason is *Schadenfreude*.

Look it up.

-a!-

I never despair whenever my glass is half-full.
I just use a really big glass.

-a!-

It doesn't matter whether the glass is half
empty or half full, the mess on the floor is
just as big either way when my children
inevitably knock it over.

-a!-

Ever notice that on social media, everyone's a
non-conformist?

At some point we must acknowledge that, if
nobody is conforming, everyone is.

-a!-

My four year old son asked a philosophical
question today. "Is 'bad' a bad word?" he
wondered.

-a!-

I think I'll have some of the hair on my chest
removed to form the words "I think, therefore I
am" so that I can wax philosophically.

-a!-

Philosophical question of the day:

Are the "You Are Here" labels on the mall maps
still there even when you're not?

-a!-

Philosophical questions through the ages.

Ancient times:
If a tree falls in the forest and there's nobody
around to hear it, does it make sound?

Modern times:
Does the light in the fridge stay on when the
door is closed?

Computer age:
Does that animated GIF continue to run when I'm
looking at a different browser window?

-a!-

KID'S ENTERTAINMENT THROUGH THE EYES OF AN ADULT

When I find myself in times of trouble, Mother Elsa seems to know. Speaking words of wisdom, *"Let it go."*

-a!-

"How do you know the berries in this bag are frozen?" asked my son this morning as I opened it.

"Listen," I replied. "You can hear them singing *'Let it Go'*."

-a!-

For every job that must be done, there is an element of fun. You find the fun and SNAP, your coworkers look at you funny.

-a!-

I'm sorry, but I just haven't trusted a single old lady since Fred and Wilma's housekeeper turned out to be *Grandma Dynamite* in disguise.

-a!-

I have it on good authority that, in the proposed sequel to *"Frozen"*, Sven will marry a regular deer and have a son named "Svenison."

-a!-

Does Ernie know that, when not appearing with him on *Sesame Street*, his rubber ducky is out chasing bears and leading convoys?

-a!-

It seems to me that the reason happy little
bluebirds can fly beyond the rainbow instead of
you is because they're birds and you're not.

-a!-

Y'know, it occurs to me that Doc can't be much
of a medical professional if he still hasn't
managed to alleviate Sneezy's allergies after 75
years.

-a!-

Rihanna.

Wasn't she one of the "Daughters of Triton" from
"The Little Mermaid?"

-a!-

I believe it was Kermit that said, "Time's fun
when you're having flies."

-a!-

If Cookie Monster sang "We've Got Tonight",
would he say "Me've got Tonight"?

-a!-

I'm 46 years old yet, when I bake, I announce
each egg as I count it in, and laugh maniacally
each time.

Thanks *Sesame Street.*

-a!-

The not-so-subtle message of the movie "Dumbo":
the best way to reveal a hidden talent is with
underage drinking.

-a!-

You'd think that, after the third or fourth
monkey falling off the bed, the doctor would
have called "Monkey Protective Services".

-a!-

"It's not easy being grain." - Kamut the Frog.

-a!-

Because of *Sesame Street's* tradition of having
the day's programming brought to you by a
different letter of the alphabet every day, I
grew up thinking that those letters were
individual corporate entities who used
advertising campaigns to buy attention.

What's worse, it was clear that some letters had
better PR than others.

-a!-

What I SHOULD have learned about life from
Disney songs:

When I send a wish towards heaven (When you wish
upon a star), I'll get the thing I most desire
(Some Day my Prince Will Come). But, if it
doesn't work out, I shouldn't worry about it
(Hakuna Matata), because everything I need will
be provided for me by the universe (The Bare
Necessities), and I should simply be happy with
who I already am instead of dreaming about being
somebody else (Under the Sea).

I say that I SHOULD have learned all that
because, off all the wisdom that I could have
gleaned from these Disney songs, all I can
really remember is that it's "better down where
it's wetter."

-a!-

MUSIC

If ever I seem distant, it's probably because,
in my head, I'm trying to figure out which *John
Williams* theme would best fit this moment

-a!-

If I've learned anything from 80s music, it's
never to whisper carelessly.

-a!-

Recently, somebody asked what life was like in
the 80s.

"Everything was pretty easy-going," I answered.
"Except the moonlight. The moonlight was very
serious."

-a!-

If your ex is walking by every time you go out
with someone new and causing you to fall to
pieces, I'd consider a restraining order.

-a!-

I want to invent a new mixed drink called
Kaleidoscope Ice.

I can see the TV commercial now: "She's there at
the barstool, the girl with *Kaleidoscope Ice*."

-a!-

If the *Society for the Promotion of Good Grammar*
gave out music awards:

The best use of the word 'moot' in a Rock Song
is: *"Jessie's Girl"*.

-a!-

If we're sending music into space, it should be
Scottish bagpipes so that aliens know that earth
is a badass and shouldn't be messed with.

-a!-

IN THE KITCHEN

Theoretically, if I have *allspice* in my pantry,
do I really need to buy any other spices?

-a!-

Do the other spices go to *sage* when they need
advice?

-a!-

How real men bake:

We don't simply beat the eggs. We utterly defeat
them.

-a!-

The recipe says to "fold in the egg whites".

Fold?

Am I baking or doing origami?

-a!-

When I label my spices, I always name whatever's
next to Ginger as "Mary-Ann".

Somehow, no matter what it is, it's still better
than Ginger.

-a!-

Kitchens should be brightly lit, if for no other
reason so as to never again mistake curry powder
for ground cinnamon.

-a!-

SHORT-SHORT STORIES

When Jethro discovered he could command
lobsters, his crime spree was short-lived when
he exclaimed "I must be dreaming. Somebody pinch
me!"

-a!-

In the dream, a loon waddled into our campsite,
sat down by the fire, and started a
conversation.

"Y'know," it began, "I'm not nearly as lonely as
most people think."

-a!-

I believe it was an Irish immigrant who coined
the expression, "the more you cry, the less you
have to pee."

You may wonder why this settler was so averse to
urination, until you consider that the saying
comes from a time when privies were unheated,
and typically situated at the end of long snowy
paths, well away from the farmhouse.

Less popular, was the expression, "Grandpa, tell
me a really sad story. It's late, and the wind
is blowing cold from the north."

-a!-

"Whoever said that it's easier to ask
forgiveness than permission," said the old man
at the bar, "never knew either of my ex-wives."

-a!-

"I don't care if we're on it at the same time.
This here page ain't big enough for the two of
us!"

-a!-

"Don't take this the wrong way," she warned.
"Because it's clearly meant as an insult."

-a!-

"I want to start taking requests," said the
fledgling performer, "but so far, the only
requests I've had are to stop singing."

-a!-

"It's simple really," she said. "I live in
constant fear that the reality fairy is going to
swoop into my life and shit all over it."

-a!-

"That cashier just gave me back more money than
I gave her," he told me. "Now that's the kind of
change I like to see in the world!"

-a!-

And, as her hair spilled languidly onto the
ground behind her head, she whispered softly, "I
will never use this hairdresser again."

-a!-

He was the first village chief to turn down the
ceremonial stallion.

Yes, that's right, he became the first ever
Horseless Headman.

-a!-

"Don't you look good," she said.

"Why?" I asked. "Is it unfair to the others?"

-a!-

"I can see right through you," she said.

"I should hope so," I countered. "You're my X-ray technician."

-a!-

"Why am you naked?" she asked wearily.

"Because sometimes," he replied indolently. "It's necessary to be bare. There's a whole Disney song about it. Look it up."

-a!-

In a dystopian future where having twins, triplets, and more was the norm, only-child Duncan was that most mythical of creatures known as the uniborn.

-a!-

"How did I die?" I asked Saint Peter.

"You thought you were being witty to a person who was smoking just outside the grocery store door, and she hit you with her car."

-a!-

ON MATH AND SCIENCE...

I live in constant fear that all those numbers I
"borrowed" from in grade school math are going
to reappear and demand I return it all with
interest.

-a!-

Einstein proved that time is relative, and moves
slower when closer to a gravity well.

This means that your head is younger than your
feet.

-a!-

Young children are like sub-atomic particles.

You can either know where they are, or how fast
they're going, but never both.

-a!-

As a physicist, Charles found weight loss
confusing. As he became more and more light, he
couldn't decide if he was more wave or particle.

-a!-

Theoretical physicists gain much insight through
deep *quantumplation*.

-a!-

Einstein's Theory of General Relativity is one
hundred years old this week.

A hundred years of relativity? Why, it seems
like only yesterday...

-a!-

It has been suggested that the decline of society began with the introduction of status bars that were unable to accurately predict the actual time remaining in a task.

-a!-

When you have to have a discussion about whether something will break-down naturally in the environment, that object is BIO-DEBATEABLE.

-a!-

If you disable the smoke detector before it senses that something on the stove is burning, you're moving faster than the speed of smoke.

-a!-

Pizza Hut is now offering a poutine pizza?

Finally, proof that when we pass through a singularity, we'll be fully aware that it's happened.

-a!-

My big statue of the number eight fell over last night and I fear that it might stay like that for infinity.

-a!-

It should be pointed out that Newton did not in fact DISCOVER gravity. He was just the first to get credit for describing its effects.

The first person to actually discover gravity was also coincidentally the first person to observe experientially that birds defecated while in flight.

-a!-

The way I understand it, the mathematical reason why it's pretty much impossible to obtain the speed of light, is that the increases in speed that are needed in order to get there are exponential. For every step along the way, your speed must be increased two-fold so that, when you're at 99.99% the speed of light, you're still only halfway there.

This might make more sense if you think about it in terms of going for a long walk with a toddler without a stroller. The closer you get to home, the slower your child moves until, eventually, they're hardly moving at all.

-a!-

Where do scientists who study optics go when they break the law?

Prism.

-a!-

ON COMICS AND SCIENCE FICTION...

Of course I choose the roads less traveled.

They're the best ones for getting my DeLorean up to 88 miles per hour.

-a!-

Idea for the name of a movie in which the hero travels back in time to kill Hitler: "Back to the Führer"

-a!-

Some people berate billionaires for not giving more to charity.

Personally, I'm more upset that none of them have used their resources to become Batman.

-a!-

I realize that I'm joining this discussion, like fifty years too late, but why isn't a man who travels through time called *"Doctor When"*?

-a!-

As I tend to stop liking things when they get too popular on social media, I feel I must bid adieu both to *Star Wars* and claiming to be an introvert.

-a!-

New Star Wars merchandise idea: tiny pieces of paper shaped like a certain bounty hunter called *"bobafetti"*.

-a!-

Should Jedi parents force-feed children who are picky eaters?

-a!-

If there's one thing I've learned from movies, it's never trust either a rope bridge or a magnetic containment field.

-a!-

"Why are Batman and Superman fighting?" asked my sons. "Was there only one scoop of ice cream left?"

-a!-

Eulogy for a spice: "Of all the souls I've encountered in my travels, his was the most ... cumin."

-a!-

So, little known fact: Darth Vader's sister Ella appeared in *Star Wars*.

That's her taking Luke and Han dressed as stormtroopers down to the detention level.

-a!-

I've been watching too much *"Doctor Who"*. I just passed gas, and could have sworn that it sounded like a Dalek.

Exterminate indeed.

-a!-

Don't disparage Darth Vader.

Insults don't sith well with him.

-a!-

The efficiency with which Star Trek transporters function seems to be inversely proportional to how much drama is needed in the plot.

-a!-

Speed was a factor in Harrison Ford's plane crash a few years back.

He was going less than 12 parsecs.

Badoom-tish

-a!-

The boys (now five) finished watching the first Star Wars trilogy.

Their conclusion: "Luke is now Dark Vader, because he has his ship."

I honestly hadn't thought of it like that.

-a!-

For Aquaman, the expression is: "Be the sea you want to change in the world."

-a!-

If money was the answer to everything, then all the denominations would be '42'.

-a!-

God grant me the serenity.

That's it. Just the *Serenity*.

Ok, maybe the cute mechanic too - in case the ship breaks down.

-a!-

Apparently, it was just plain old
califragilisticexpialidocious until it was
exposed to radioactive material and developed
powers and abilities far beyond those of mortal
words.

-a!-

What does Lois Lane wear to bed when she's not
in the mood?

Her Kryptonightie.

-a!-

If the Borg tried to assimilate a medieval
village, would they say, "Resistance is feudal"?

-a!-

Today, my eldest son saw an older boy who looked
just like him.

"Look Daddy," he said. "It's me, visiting myself
from the future!"

-a!-

This morning, the boys were both standing at the
toilet peeing when one of them said, "Don't
cross the streams!"

I love my geeky sons.

-a!-

One of my twin sons just looked at his brother
and said, "Are you me from the future?"

I am one proud geeky dad.

-a!-

I'm almost as old as both the *Doctor Who* and
James Bond franchises, who are still going
strong.

Of course, they've both been rebooted a few
times, but that's beside the point.

-a!-

Online, as in life, don't be troll, be a rabbit;
they're far more dangerous.

-a!-

I don't know if the best things in life are
free, but they certainly appear to be British.
#montypython, #doctorwho, #harrypotter, #lotr,
#beatles.

-a!-

You can learn a lot from Supervillains.

No matter how soundly they've been defeated, no
matter how close to death they are, no matter
how many times they've failed before, they
always try again - ALWAYS.

Now that's a role model to believe in!

-a!-

Time traveler's motto: don't put off today what
can be done yesterday.

-a!-

Time travelers get more done by yesterday's
breakfast than most people do tomorrow.

-a!-

ON HEALTH CONCERNS

I haven't been online much of late as I have, quite literally, been playing with my testicles instead.

Now lest you think I jest, I'm only telling you this because I found a lump on one of my testicles last week. The doctor examined it the other day, and is of the opinion that it's nothing to be concerned about (in fact, it's already shrinking), but an ultrasound next week will say for sure. Apparently, testicles are notoriously lumpy to begin with, and only 4 in 100 such growths turn out to be cancerous.

In any event, I remain grateful for the perspective that this experience has given me, especially this close to the holiday season. It has also given me a renewed respect for those with genuine health concerns.

Now, at the risk of sounding even more inappropriately juvenile than usual, I close this post with a request of my fellow males to promote testicular health:

Play with you balls, boys.

Play with your balls.

-a!-

LIVE-BLOGGING MY COLONOSCOPY

I've a routine colonoscopy tomorrow, so for the next thirty hours, I've been told that I can only consume food that I can see through.

Naturally, I'm going to take it on faith that this includes bacon that is sliced REALLY thin.

-a!-

Hour 2 of the colonoscopy fast. Have the clouds always looked like hot dogs?

-a!-

Hour 4 of the fast and I'm preparing my witty banter for tomorrow's colonoscopy.

Surely, there's an anal probe joke the Doctor hasn't heard, right?

-a!-

Hour 6 of my colonoscopy fast and I'm being told that the salad I had been looking forward to is actually SALAX which is Latin for "portal to the netherworld."

-a!-

JELLO IS NOT FOOD!

If you can't put it on a stick and dip it in mayo, then it's not food.

-a!-

Hour 10 of the colonoscopy fast. Apparently, I can eat (drink) broth, but not if I batter it and deep fry it first.

-a!-

Hour 11 of my colonoscopy fast and delirium has set in. There's a dead relative in the corner of the room beckoning me into the light.

Normally I'd refuse to go, but he's holding a cheeseburger.

-a!-

Ah Good Morning to my liquid breakfast of champions: SALAX.

Apparently, it's specially designed for athletes who like to run.

-a!-

Hour 25 of the colonoscopy fast.

I'm being told that this fast used to be three days.

That might be one of the reasons some old people are so bitter.

-a!-

Hour 29, and I'm off to the hospital having taken Deadpool's advice, and have worn my brown pants.

-a!-

I've been given an ID bracelet. I asked for one for the other wrist too so that I could cosplay as Wonder Woman, but she apparently thought I was only joking.

-a!-

It's 2016, and yet hospital gowns still don't have cell phone pockets.

-a!-

I don't see any "no selfies" sign in the
outpatients room, so I'm going to assume that
we're good to go.

-a!-

Apparently fully aware of how difficult it is to
say "anaesthesiologist", he was introduced to me
as the "sleepy-time man."

-a!-

I'm sitting in a recovery room where I'm being
encouraged to fart.

Encouraged to fart?

Did I die on the table and go to heaven?

-a!-

The results are in.

I'm pleased to tell my Conservative friends that
the Doctor did NOT find my head while performing
the colonoscopy.

-a!-

MILLION DOLLAR IDEAS!

Best ever name for a car repair business:

Auto Correct.

-a!-

Glow in the dark tags.

So that I can tell which way my shirt is
supposed to go when I'm getting dressed in the
dark.

-a!-

A toaster that sends out a signal when it's
being used that temporarily disables the nearest
smoke detector.

-a!-

A portable debit machine that has a magnetic
reader on BOTH sides of the slot so that the
cashier doesn't have to tell every customer that
they're swiping their card the wrong way.

-a!-

Bubble wrap filled with helium instead of air so
that when you wrap things and mail them, your
shipping costs are reduced.

-a!-

A system where the customer service agent that
you've just called doesn't have to ask for your
account number AFTER you've already entered it
using your phone.

-a!-

A handicap door-opening button on the double
doors that lead into malls and office buildings
that opens BOTH doors at roughly the same time,
one just after the other.

Because, really, who needs to only open one?

Are there people who only want to go as far as
the vestibule in between the two doors, and just
stay there?

-a!-

ON SPIDERS...

A very large primeval spider has been spotted
lurking about the garden shed.

I think it might be part dragon, because it's
covered in bony plates that slide noisily
against each other when it moves.

That's it. We might just as well board the shed
up. I'm never going in there again.

                    -a!-

Apparently Jesus Christ has come back to earth
as that giant hairy spider over there, because
that's the name everyone is calling it by when
they see it.

                    -a!-

That spider was so big, that after one smack
with the fly swatter, he just looked at me and
said, "That all you got, boy?"

                    -a!-

I'm thinking of re-writing *Life of Pi* so that
it takes place in a canoe and - instead of a
tiger - the hero is trapped there with a wolf
spider.

                    -a!-

This is the time of year when spiders emerge, so
make sure that there is lots of spider-friendly
things for them to feed on.

Like insects, small dogs, puppies, kittens, and
unattended infants.

Oh, and nightmares. Don't forget them. Spiders
LOVE to feed on your nightmares.

-a!-

Note to self: never tell your children that a
male mosquito is actually a spider with wings.

-a!-

The other day, my wife spotted a big hairy
spider by the TV. I never saw it, but it must
have been huge if her reaction was any
indication.

"Quick!" she yelled, clearly alarmed, as if the
spider was threatening the very lives of the
twins, "Give me your shoe!"

Immediately, I started for the vestibule by the
back door where we keep the shoes, but then
hesitated.

"Wait!" I wondered, suddenly remembering my
arachnophobia. "Why does it have to be MY shoe?"

-a!-

To help my sons with their fear of spiders, I
let one crawl on me just now.

If anyone needs me, I'll be screaming into a
pillow.

-a!-

Is there a name for the irrational fear of
tomato stems because they kinda look like
spiders?

-a!-

There's a spider in the bathroom.

Anyone know how to make one of those homemade
flame thrower thingees?

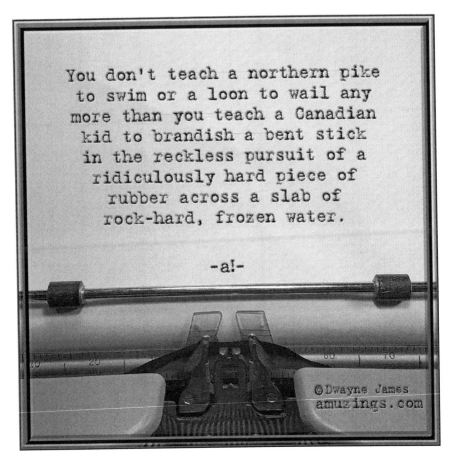

You don't teach a northern pike
to swim or a loon to wail any
more than you teach a Canadian
kid to brandish a bent stick
in the reckless pursuit of a
ridiculously hard piece of
rubber across a slab of
rock-hard, frozen water.

-al-

©Dwayne James
amuzings.com

HOCKEY OWES ME AN APOLOGY
It's a Hate Affair for the Ages

I really hate hockey.

There, I said it.

Now, before somebody tries to use this confession as grounds to revoke my Canadian citizenship, let me explain: it's hockey's fault. Oh, and maybe Tarzan's too.

My hate affair with hockey is kind of ironic actually. In truth, I should be one of the game's biggest fans. I did, after all, grow up in *Cochrane, Ontario,* the birthplace of **Tim Horton**, arguably our nation's most famous hockey player, thanks in large part to his posthumous consecration as this country's most venerated peddler of highly addictive caffeinated beverages and deep-fried breakfast substitutes.

Yet, in spite of this most excellent pedigree, hockey and I never saw eye to facemask.

It's not like I didn't try either. When, at the tender age of nine, I joined a children's hockey league at my father's behest, it was ostensibly to learn how to play the game. Little did I know though that, in Canada — at least in the 1970s — you did not join a children's hockey league at the tender age of nine to *learn* how to play hockey.

No! You were a Canadian boy; hockey was supposed to be in your *blood!* You didn't teach a northern pike to swim or a loon to wail any more than you taught a Canadian kid to brandish a bent stick in the reckless pursuit of a ridiculously hard piece of rubber across a slab of rock-hard, frozen water.

The problem for me was that, in my childhood, I had been mostly oblivious to the Canadian hockey culture that had permeated so much of that era. Oh sure, I was aware that, sometime in my recent past, some guy named **Henderson** had single-handedly prolonged the cold war, and some other guy named **Bobby Howe** (or something) was every kid's hero. And I also knew that a lot of boys my age liked *Les Canadiens*, a team from a province that, at the time, didn't even want to *be* Canadien.

But that was about all I knew. That's why I was surprised just as much as the next **Guy Lafleur** when, one cold Saturday morning in December, my father dragged me away from the television where I had been watching a classic Tarzan movie, and told me that I was going to play hockey. I was reluctant to go, but at least he wasn't threatening to take me hunting again. I think we can all agree that his idea the previous autumn of getting behind the prey to flush it through the forest in the direction of a frightened kid with a loaded firearm had been a bad idea.

Yeah, the 1970s was a tough time to be a child.

If today's parents hover too closely, then their counterparts in the 1970s were floating entirely off-planet. I'm not sure where our parents spent the majority of their time in the seventies, but it certainly wasn't actually spending time with us or answering our questions. As kids, we were forced to figure out far too many things on our own, a problem that was exacerbated in subjects that adults avoided at the best of times—like sex for instance.

You might think that I'm exaggerating this last part, but I'm not. When I was about ten years old—when most of my friends were out watching *Star Wars*—I saw an educational movie on the CBC that promised to answer all my questions about how babies were made. I was excited at the prospect. I had a *lot* of questions.

Now, I hadn't been expecting pornography, but I *had* hoped that a film about sexual reproduction might have at least elucidated the mechanics involved. Instead, the narrator vaguely explained that babies came about as the eventual result of a part of the male anatomy that "fits together *really* well" with a part of the female anatomy. Unfortunately, the movie failed to specify what those parts were, much less how they actually fit together.

Perhaps predictably, it was just a few days later when I accidentally stuck a finger into the ear of one of my female classmates and couldn't help but notice how well these two parts of our anatomies fit together. Had I impregnated her? Who knew? I had, quite literally, never been told differently.

And so, in this spirit of forcing me to figure things out by myself, my father introduced me to our *Great National Pastime* by dropping me off at the Tim Horton Memorial arena in Cochrane, and then promptly driving away. I was met at the door by complete strangers who ushered me inside, covered me in pads that were held in place by elastics thicker than the kind you find on clumps of broccoli, strapped dangerously sharp pieces of metal to my feet, gave me an L-shaped stick, and pushed me out onto the ice where I spun around a few times before eventually coming to a stop, thanks to a force I would later find out was called "friction." (Friction, I might add, became one of my best friends in high school, despite the fact that the aforementioned educational movie had failed to even mention it.)

Then, those same strangers who had just abandoned me in the middle of the hockey rink, and who were allegedly supposed to be teaching me how to actually play the game that I'd just suited up for, had the temerity to yell at me for not knowing what to do next.

I was at least aware enough to know that the activity in which I was forcibly engaged, involved something called a "puck." The *Peter the Puck* cartoons — the only part of Hockey Night in Canada I ever watched beyond the theme song — told me as much.

But, what was I supposed to do with it?

Was I supposed to put the puck in a net? If so, then which one? There were, after all, two to choose from, and I had the distinct impression that the red-faced guy with the angry vein on his forehead might take offense if I chose poorly.

I sighed. When I had left home that morning, Tarzan had been on his way to New York City. I would have liked to have seen how that movie ended.

I was supposed to be chasing the puck, the angry man with the now-purple face told me before hurling a few insults, including some kind of insinuation that my parents had never been married.

Chase the puck? But why? Every time I went anywhere near it, the other kids would push me down and skate away with it. Who needed that kind of stress? Why was I even playing a game that encouraged this kind of violence? Did my Mom know about this?

More to the point, why couldn't I just buy my own puck so that I wouldn't have to share it with kids who thought that shoving each other to the ice was a fun way to spend a Saturday morning? Then, I could take my new puck, lay down on the floor of my recroom and roll it around while I watched Tarzan. Where the room was warm. Where the floor was carpeted. If I was going to spend so much time prone on a surface while I played with a puck, then that surface should at least be carpeted.

As I lay on the ice during that first game and looked up at the rafters of my hometown ice rink, I wondered if Tim Horton had ever seen this view. I toyed with the idea of getting up, but it seemed kinda pointless if I was only going to be pushed back down again, and things were certainly a lot less chaotic there at the end of the rink where the puck wasn't.

After the "game", we were herded into a change room that was — I was disappointed to discover — already full of pre-teen boys who were not being supervised by adults. In case you are not already aware of it, let me be the first to tell you that pre-teen boys who are not being supervised by adults are little *shits*. I found that out the hard way that morning when one of those hoodlums blew a huge lungful of cigarette smoke directly into my face after telling me that I was in the wrong change room because I played hockey like a girl.

Looking back, I would personally like to thank that little thug for forcing me to inhale such a large quantity of a well-known carcinogen. He single-handedly helped me to discover that smoking was bad for my health by making me forget how to breathe. For, like, an hour.

Coincidentally, that same boy also taught me never to be a bully, because I had just discovered first-hand that being bullied sucks. Almost as much as hockey.

That was my last time on the ice. I decided right then and there that, until hockey apologized, it was dead to me.

The next Saturday morning, I was back watching Tarzan.

The long-overdue hockey apology, I'm going to assume, is forthcoming.

-a!-

A Postscript:

*Now, speaking of hockey apologies, this story gave me an idea for a reality TV show called **"The Great Hockey Apology."***

I know that I'm not alone in having been bullied out of hockey at a young age. Since posting this story online, I've heard from scores of people who had similar experiences, many of them involving real assholes for coaches. For many people growing up in the 70s, being bullied for being different was a way of life for lots of things besides just sports.

So, I'd love to see a reality TV show that gathers a bunch of these adults who, like me when they were kids, wanted to like hockey but were never given the chance. Then, these participants would be taken to a real hockey camp and taught how to play the right way by famous hockey players. There'd be lots of interviews with the players and the officials, all with the goal of driving the point home that bullying is bad.

In the final episode, the new team would be given a chance to play on a real NHL rink with a real NHL team. Then, some official from the NHL would come out on the ice and offer each of the players an apology on behalf of hockey.

So there's my idea internet.

Run with it.

Make it happen.

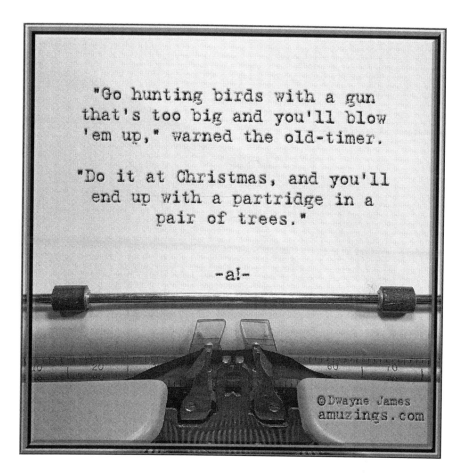

"Go hunting birds with a gun
that's too big and you'll blow
'em up," warned the old-timer.

"Do it at Christmas, and you'll
end up with a partridge in a
pair of trees."

-a!-

©Dwayne James
amuzings.com

AH, CHRISTMAS
'Tis the Season to Indecently Impale Angels on Top of Evergreens

Ah, December.

Let the bitter arguments over how to express
messages of peace and love begin.

-a!-

And here I thought every season was the season
to be jolly.

-a!-

My son is making out his Xmas list, and just asked us how to spell "sex".

"What?" my wife asked, incredulous.

"Sex," he repeated. "As in LEGO sets."

"What a relief," I whispered to my wife. "For a moment I thought he and I were asking for the same thing for Christmas."

-a!-

As the family ate Christmas dinner with the father who had just faked his death to get them there, they remembered that the reason they had cut him out of their lives was his predilection for extreme manipulative emotional blackmail.

-a!-

As the family ate Christmas dinner with the father who had just faked his own death to get them there, they fondly remembered the last time they had gathered like this, shortly after the death of their mother.

"Wait," thought Klaus the eldest son. "Did she actually die of natural causes, or did the old man kill her to get us all together?"

-a!-

Birthdays that occur close to Christmas always sound violent because they always seem to be described as "Christmas-slash-birthday".

-a!-

If every day could be just like Christmas, oh when would my children sleep?

-a!-

All the silver bells seem to say "throw cares
away."

What? Are they playing "Hakuna Matata" or
something?

-a!-

Just wondering, of all the books like the Grinch
that preach that "Christmas doesn't come from a
store", how many have price tags?

-a!-

Wrapping gifts?

Here's a tip: Wrapping paper with horizontal
stripes will make your gifts look bigger than
they actually are.

-a!-

I only regret I have but one digestive system to
give to this most excellent Christmas dinner.

-a!-

My son is making out his Xmas list, and just
asked me how to spell *"Hatchimal"*.

My response: "It's spelled
N-E-V-E-R-G-O-N-N-A-H-A-P-P-E-N"

-a!-

I have an electric knife, but I prefer to carve
the turkey the way my forefathers did: drunk.

-a!-

In an effort to remove innuendo from Xmas
carols, I changed it to:
"Santa Claus is *Going* to Town."

I dunno, but it just seems worse somehow.

-a!-

This season, the fact that fruit will come
packaged inside cake I'm sure will in no way
diminish its nutritive value.

-a!-

There's a ghost hanging out in the living room
this Christmas.

Well waddyaknow. It's a presence under the tree.

-a!-

What does Santa say when he's swimming?

H_2O H_2O H_2O .

-a!-

You realize of course that, if I were in charge
of Christmas, I'd call them "dwayne-deer."

-a!-

"I'm pretty sure he's still a burglar even if he
leaves things behind," is apparently not an
argument kids want to hear this time of year.

-a!-

Where is the country of "Orientar" anyways, and
why does it have three kings?

-a!-

There, but for the grace of my winter tires,
go I.

-a!-

*This one was shortlisted for a CBC twistmas
tweet contest in Dec, 2013*

Frosty hated his Winter Wonderland, living in
constant fear of the roving bands of kiddies who
were intent on knocking him down.

-a!-

Who advented Christmas?

-a!-

There was a time before the twins when my
favourite carol was *Silent Night.*

Now a silent night is *All I want for Christmas.*

-a!-

Apparently Christmas TV movies are an
opportunity to find out that your favourite 80s
actors and actresses are still around.

-a!-

My grown-up Christmas wish?

The toys I asked for as a kid but never got.

I'm still keeping track Santa.

-a!-

"Tiny tots with their eyes all aglow"?

Crickey! Is it a Christmas carol or a horror
movie?

-a!-

At Christmas dinner a few years back, somebody gave a mid-meal toast saying that there was a little Santa in each of us.

"*Wait. What?*" I interrupted. "I thought this was ham."

-a!-

At around noon on Boxing Day, my seven year-old son asked if we could call Santa to thank him.

"Not right now," I answered. "He'll still be sleeping after being up all night."

"Why? Is he a vampire?"

-a!-

The double-entendres make sense,
The innuendos become clear,
When you sing carols about a man,
Who comes but once a year.

-a!-

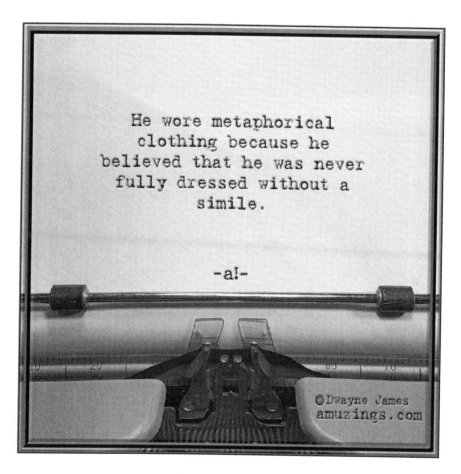

He wore metaphorical clothing because he believed that he was never fully dressed without a simile.

-a!-

©Dwayne James
amuzings.com

WORDPLAY
Teaching Old Words New Tricks

My excellent attention to detial is surpassed only by my love of irony.

-a!-

People who refuse to see the truth won't take know for an answer.

-a!-

The future. It's the new now.

-a!-

Ironically, the only way to truly express the fact that words have failed you is with words.

-a!-

It's beyond me why an alternate name for a "mariner" isn't "nautician."

-a!-

Goodbyes that are abruptly cut short end without further adieu.

-a!-

Lately, my favourite music is the sweet tune nestled right in the middle of the word "opportunity."

-a!-

Whenever I have a song stuck in my head, I'm sure not to engage in dangerous activities.

I don't want to die with the music inside of me.

-a!-

I'm going to start celebrating the Sabbath on Fridays simply so that I can start saying, "Thank Friday it's God".

-a!-

I'm not exactly sure what hearsay is, but apparently a friend of a friend claims to know.

-a!-

When somebody says, "Word," I can't help myself,
and reply, "Association."

-a!-

So, apparently the thimble game piece in
Monopoly is not meant to be used as the item it
represents.

It's merely *thimbolic*.

-a!-

Heh.

It just occurred to me that when you go to
school to become a cop, you're turning yourself
into the police.

-a!-

People who indulge in dangerous flights of fancy
like to go out on a whim.

-a!-

People who don't know the definitions of words
are living beyond their means.

-a!-

One could say that, when somebody makes a dick-
move as expected, it was totally *predicktable*.

-a!-

Suddenly, there was a LOL in the conversation...

-a!-

That song was so bad that I'm calling it the
crime of the sensory.

-a!-

People who retire with an overabundance of the
fifth letter of the alphabet live a life of
'E's.

-a!-

I've heard of college kids putting ex-lax into
the food of a roommate they didn't like.

With friends like that, who needs enemas?

-a!-

Attractive singers have better *acutestics.*

-a!-

I like the surreal as much as the next chicken.

-a!-

If you keep avoiding your bills, you're
overdueing it.

-a!-

Sweaters that don't have a front or back, and
fit around the neck the same either way, are
ambineckstrous.

-a!-

I'd always assumed that "muchas gracias" meant
"big lawn".

-a!-

When you do something more than twice, you
"overtwo" it.

-a!-

If you celebrate Thanksgiving by expressing
doubt and uncertainty about the coming year,
you're actually celebrating something called
"misgiving".

-a!-

"I was being followed. Always behind me, and
slightly to the right. They were my five o'clock
shadow."

-a!-

The other day, a friend called while I was
sketching a human figure.

"I'll have to call you back," I said. "I'm
figuratively in the middle of doing something."

-a!-

The medium will truly be the message the moment
that a mime becomes a meme.

-a!-

I woke up this morning, and my thumbs were
arguing.

They're taking this opposable thing a little too
far.

-a!-

Nuts, I broke another tomato.

Somebody hand me the tomato paste so I can glue
it back together.

-a!-

One typo can make all the difference in the
word.

-a!-

What's a simile? Is it like an Italian sausage
or something?

-a!-

At my house on Oct 31, kids have to answer
Grammar trivia in order to get candy.

I call it *Vowelleen.*

-a!-

Did you know that there is no baseball in Hell?

Apparently all the bats are out of there.

-a!-

How do you say chocolate backwards? Lot-a-chock.

-a!-

It's a little known fact that Z used to be the
first letter of the alphabet instead of A.

They had to move Z because it was allergic to
B's.

-a!-

I've said it before, and I'll say it again: "I
don't like to repeat myself."

-a!-

Ever notice that the word "negotiation" ends
with a "no" that's been turned around?

-a!-

Excellent title for a horror novel about a rogue
genie: "A Wish to Build a Scream On."

You're welcome internet.

-a!-

For things called "hangers," they sure spend a
lot of time on the floor of the closet not
actually hanging.

-a!-

For a blog about things that are uniquely
Canadian, here's my suggestion for the title:
Canadian Specific

-a!-

There's got to be a joke in the term "standing
ovulation", but I just can't see it now.

I'll have to get back to you on it.

-a!-

Ten times that top ten lists disappointed:

10. Right now

-a!-

Ironically, since being written by *Heraclitus* in
500 B.C., the phrase "The only thing that is
constant is change" has remained the same.

-a!-

Sentient potatoes be like, "I think, therefore I
yam."

-a!-

Ever notice that the alphabet is grammatically
incorrect in the first three letters?

It should be A IS C.

-a!-

"Open up the windows to get a cross-breeze
going," she said.

Am I the only one who is uncomfortable making
the wind angry?

-a!-

"But I was always real," protested shit.

-a!-

Never one to be left out, pee would like to
remind everyone that it happens too.

-a!-

I don't call it "shaving my head". I prefer to
call it a "comb-under".

-a!-

"I never knew my father," said Invention. "My
mother said it wasn't necessary. How ironic. "

-a!-

How best to describe meal time in a house with
toddler twins: *sittus interruptus*.

-a!-

I love wheat too much to give it up, so am thinking of going on the *glutton-free* diet instead.

-a!-

I saw a play in an *apatheatre* the other day.

Nobody clapped.

-a!-

I get very emotional when I realize that I've never truly understood the meaning of the word "pathos".

-a!-

I'm thinking of opening a small motel that caters to anti-social clientele.

I'm going to call it an "Out".

-a!-

In Toronto just after the ice storm I happened to see some prostitutes out walking their dogs, so I quipped, "Let slip the dogs of whores."

-a!-

Unspoken objections are not only moot, they're also mute.

-a!-

I'm batting around a couple of ideas for the title of my auto-biography.

It's a toss-up between *"A Brief Time of History"* or *"The Relativity of Theory"*.

-a!-

Dear Abby, my employee just accused me of
micro-management.

How do I tell her that she doesn't need the
hyphen?

-a!-

If things always happen for a reason, and yet
always happen in threes then can it be said that
things happen for a *threason*?

-a!-

Thank you. Your joke amuses my bouche.

-a!-

I'm thinking of changing my name to "It" so that
happy people who know me can clap their hands.

-a!-

Earth without art is just "eh."

So, it's Canadian?

-a!-

Rejoice.

Because apparently the first joice didn't take.

-a!-

When a guide dog keeps their person away from
danger, that person says, "There but for the
grace of dog go I."

-a!-

With respect to you Sir Elton, in my experience,
rolling thunder under the covers isn't nearly as
romantic as you make it sound.

-a!-

What's another way of describing an umbrella?

Think of it as a "get out of hail free card."

-a!-

All this time, I thought #Brexit was the final
meal that a yuppie ate just prior to a lunchtime
execution.

-a!-

I always thought that the phrase "Art Thou" was
a command to do something creative.

-a!-

Ever notice that there's no direct synonym for
the word "procrastinator"?

Apparently, *Roget* said he'd get around to it
later.

-a!-

Today, I celebrate the fact that, after years of
leaving so many things unfinished, I have
reached a point in my life where I finish what I

-a!-

If there were a church for people who lacked
proper respect and were never serious, then I'd
be the *irreverand.*

-a!-

My secret to looking good naked? I always wear
my glasses.

I'm sorry. I'm being told that should read
"seeing well while naked".

-a!-

How are *Cheerios* made anyhow?

They look suspiciously deep-fried.

-a!-

Tonight's symphony, performed entirely by
tapping on various pieces of wood, is called
"Eine Kleine Knock Music".

-a!-

Even if I did want to have more children, that
snip has sailed.

-a!-

I'm determined to make the world a more positive
place, so from now on, I'm calling it *Yesvember*.

-a!-

I used to be able to ramble on for hours, but
now I find that, as I age, I've got really poor
digression.

-a!-

So, apparently "viscosity" is not in fact a
measurement as to how brutal and ferocious a
person is.

Go figure.

-a!-

All this time, I thought a woodwind was the act
of passing gas in the forest.

-a!-

When casting magic spells, it helps to speak a
magic word.

I use *Ava Cado*.

-a!-

When I'm nervous, I tend to mix up words that
are similar, which is why I'll never give a
public speech on the joys of frequent
meditation.

-a!-

You know you've looked at too many technical
drawings when you see "What To Do in Case of A
Fire", and wonder what to do in case of B fire.

-a!-

I've found that we are often ourselves guilty of
that which we blame others for.

Which is why I take issue with how many talented
and handsome people I know.

-a!-

So many seem surprised when, after a political
revolution, they're right back where they
started.

Funny, I thought that was what a revolution was.

-a!-

A musical note that lasts forever is *etonal*.

-a!-

Let's be honest and tell it like it is. That thing on the front of old trains isn't a cow catcher.

It's really a *cow plow.*

-a!-

I woke up from a dream of angels singing this morning.

I'm taking it as a sing from above.

-a!-

On nights where I wake up inside my dreams, I like to say that I'm wide asleep.

-a!-

When a person has to make a phone call but keeps putting it off, they're post-phoning it.

-a!-

Watch your step around the light fantastic.

-a!-

I've just created a new smiley icon that uses silent letters and characters. I'm using it now.

-a!-

Just who is "Lest" anyway? And why isn't he allowed to judge?

-a!-

Overheard conversation:

"What's that flock of crows doing over there?"

"It's a murder."

"What? Really? That's terrible! Somebody should call the Police."

-a!-

Wind Chill Factor:

Proof once and for all that it's never about how things actually are, it's about how you feel about them.

-a!-

I've always wondered: when did being full of awe turn into awful?

-a!-

A comma is just a period with a skid mark.

The sentence tried to stop, but couldn't, so it just kept going instead.

-a!-

If you have a blog or twitter feed that caters to procrastinators, you should consider calling it *"The newslater"*.

-a!-

It occurs to me that people who really have their shit together should probably be eating more fibre.

-a!-

It was when I flunked out of high-school English
that I realized that words had finally failed
me.

-a!-

Actions are spoken louder than words.

Unless they use the passive voice.

Then, they're pretty much the same volume.

-a!-

He only avoided certain people.

He was an "exclusive reclusive".

-a!-

Not known for his subtlety, his way of fishing
for compliments involved dynamite and a big net.

-a!-

I don't speak to my hair anymore; we had a
falling out.

-a!-

An argument over who can better secure a jar lid
is a CLASH OF THE TIGHTENS!

-a!-

When creative writers argue with each other,
there are always two stories to every side.

-a!-

The other night, I'm pretty sure I heard the detective on TV say that he was going to dust for "sphincter prints".

Just what kind of crime scene was it?

-a!-

Molten rock burns paper and melts scissors.

I win!

-a!-

Appropriately, before I could do the top-secret work for the cookie company, I had to sign a wafer.

-a!-

If you were paying spousal support to a minister or someone in a religious order, would it be called *sanctimony?*

-a!-

When Tim's changed the sizes of its coffees, it shifted all the cups one size smaller:

The medium is the message, although it used to be the large.

-a!-

Pity the poor homophobe, whose threat to kick the gay man's ass was changed by way of a typo of karmic proportions into an offer to lick it.

-a!-

Did you know that hummingbirds always start their correspondence with: "To hum it may concern..."

-a!-

Some phone services will ask if you want French
by telling you to "fait le deux" which,
literally translated is "make number two".

Surely there's an easier way?

-a!-

Dear Kris Kristofferson. I just noticed that my
Thesaurus doesn't list "freedom" as a synonym
for "nothing left to lose."

You lied.

-a!-

"One day, I will be like my father and represent
a society without government or law," said @.

-a!-

ONLINE QUIZ: Are you self-involved?

QUESTION 1: Is this post about you?

If you said yes, you are. If not, you're in
denial, because it actually is.

-a!-

Poets don't get angry, they get pithed off.

-a!-

Ironically, nobody saw it coming when Mr. and
Mrs. Voyant named their first-born daughter
"Claire".

-a!-

Vests are magical. Think about it.

In a marriage ceremony, it's where the
official's power comes from during the
pronouncement.

-a!-

When monkeys lose the ability to grip things
with their tails, it is known as "posthensile
tail syndrome."

-a!-

Before I opened the email, I knew somehow that
it was about an upcoming sale.

I guess I had a promonition!

-a!-

There are some lines you just don't cross.

Others become 't's and 'x's.

-a!-

Who's got three thumbs and was recently exposed
to radioactive material?

-a!-

Too many commas put a sentence to sleep,
rendering it (don't tell me you didn't see this
coming) commatose.

-a!-

The two men had met at the Supervillain academy
some twenty odd years ago as youths, and
promised to be best fiends forever.

-a!-

I must have slept funny last night, because I
woke up laughing.

-a!-

All this time, I thought a *perennial* was a part
of the human anatomy.

-a!-

Due to cost of living increases, we regret to
announce that our range eggs are no longer free.

-a!-

If they ever take roosters on the space shuttle,
will they be known as "*shuttlecocks?*"

-a!-

I don't swear much, but when I do it's usually
to stress how fucking blessed I am to have such
godamned amazing friends and family.

-a!-

I know what you were trying to say, but "phallic
victory" was pretty funny.

-a!-

If you ask questions while standing in a line,
you're engaging in a little queue and A.

-a!-

Y'know, the internet used to meme something.

-a!-

For years, I thought that the French word for a good wind was "'vla."

-a!-

I want to cook up some happy soup, but first I need a laughing stock.

-a!-

Personally, I prefer the term *Batshit Happy.*

-a!-

Like I know what a simile is.

-a!-

For some reason, the legumes in my garden didn't grow last year.

Not a day goes by that I don't wonder what might have bean.

-a!-

Beware. Beans are a mung us.

-a!-

Hey, you. Get offa my clown...

Wait. That might be wrong.

-a!-

It's a well-known fact that, when tartan parents have children, they're rewarded with the pitter-pattern of little feet.

-a!-

When you write something that sees both sides of
a topic, it is *bitextual*.

-a!-

Pick up the peace:

What we should be saying when cease-fire talks
aren't proceeding quickly enough.

-a!-

While what you said was technically correct, I
think what you meant to say was:

"The *onus* is on you."

With an 'o.'

Not an 'a.'

-a!-

So, if you eat so much fruit that it goes right
through you and cleans you out, it's called a
bananema.

-a!-

When forced to choose between a couple of people
impersonating the "King", I usually select the
lesser of the two Elvis.

-a!-

Am I really here?

Apparently not, at least according to the
sensors that activate the taps and the towels in
public washrooms.

-a!-

The Helveticas, they are a changin'.

-a!-

I've never understood fractions. They only make
sense to me 9/10s of the time.

-a!-

Following the example of the popular acronyms
"J.Lo" and "J.Law", would the short form for
Peanut Butter be "P.Butt"?

-a!-

I used to have some really bad habits, but they
suddenly switched to their exact opposites.

It was a *vice versa*.

-a!-

Personally, I prefer to watch like nobody's
dancing, and listen like nobody's singing.

-a!-

I love when a really bad writer's block finally
breaks.

It feels like... um ...

Well, damn.

-a!-

I don't like idle gossip.

I prefer it to be running at full throttle
thank-you-very-much.

-a!-

Ever notice how often erotic literature mentions
horses that are hung?

I thought that, traditionally, you euthanized a
horse by shooting it.

-a!-

Don't forget that there's a fine line between
being inane and being insane.

It's right after the 1st 'n'; the one that's
shaped like an 's'.

-a!-

Or, as my own coming of age story was known in
my family, "Who has Smelt the Wind?"

-a!-

The new Star Wars film, where Han and Chewie go
on their first adventure, is called "*Solo*", and
not, as I suggested: "*When Hairy met Solo.*"

-a!-

Of big cats in captivity, the following can be
said:

In the lion, the mighty lion, the jungle sleeps
tonight.

-a!-

It occurs to me that "Mommy Long-legs" sounds a
lot more sexist than the Daddy version.

-a!-

Some e-mails invoke an involuntary burst of emotion in me, or a contraction of my facial muscles.

Naturally, I store them in my *spasm* folder.

-a!-

Deceased authors are read to me.

-a!-

A retro stuffed animal that doesn't talk, and is hilariously rude to people: Mr. Beanie Baby

-a!-

There's a new bug going around that causes a rash on major arm joints.

It's called the elbowa virus.

-a!-

Ergo, a logical conclusion that is ugly and backwards is a real ogre.

-a!-

Driving around rural roads, it's clear that "Firewood" is the most popular name for camps.

-a!-

I saw a coin on the ground yesterday.

"Carpe Dime!" I called out as I seized it.

-a!-

I just *tuckled* the boys in which is, in case you're wondering, half tuck and half tickle.

-a!-

Whenever I hear the word "Spanish", I naturally
assume that it means a language that's kinda
close to "Span."

-a!-

"It was the cheese fondue what exploded," said
the old man. "You could tell by the de-brie
field."

Perhaps predictably, nobody laughed.

-a!-

In a universe of opposites, problems simply
cannot exist without solutions.

That's why one of my favourite expressions is
"Ah, the utility of it all!"

-a!-

Arguing with binary sales reps is the worst.
They don't take ON for an answer.

-a!-

Horses that move in a circular direction to the
left are going canter-clockwise.

-a!-

In the French and Spanish languages, nouns can
be either male or female.

What, no trans nouns? Seems pretty close-minded
to me.

-a!-

You are what you eat.

That's why I start each day with a big bowl of "Lucky and Charming" cereal.

-a!-

You are what you eat. That's why I start each morning with a huge smoothie.

-a!-

I've heard the expression "always leave others wanting more," but as an introvert, I always want others leaving more.

-a!-

Sometimes, the mysterious works in lordly ways.

-a!-

We're getting rid of a few of our extra dictionaries today in preparation for our big move.

I hope it's a desision that dusn't come bak too bite us on the as.

-a!-

I cannot begin to tell you how frustrating it is to have misplaced your thesaurus after a big move.

-a!-

I like taking a jar of olives, chopping them up into little pieces, and calling it a jar of *"someofs"*.

-a!-

Silhouetto.

What's that? A shadow of a lady's high heel
shoe?

-a!-

New fairy tale idea: a blind girl falls in love
and immediately regains the ability to see.

It's called *"Sight at First Love."*

-a!-

Frankly, my dear?

I thought her name was Scarlett, not Frankly.

-a!-

I'm thinking of taking a nanny with me outside
to paint.

It will be plein air with an au pair.

-a!-

I want to open a restaurant that gives out
predictions for the future along with the
sandwiches.

It will be called: *"Oracle at Deli."*

-a!-

Do you realize that, if you rearrange the
letters in the phrase, "I don't know what an
anagram is" it spells the word, "bunny?"

-a!-

Breakfast in French sounds like a meal you've
already eaten.

-a!-

Little known fact:

If you shudder in pleasure while cleaning your
ear with a Q-tip, it's called an "aurgasm."

-a!-

I'm thinking of putting a picture of Sally Field
on a fidget spinner and calling it a "Gidget
Spinner".

-a!-

The hottest marital aid this time of the year is
green and shaped like an evergreen.

It's called the Christmas 'O' Tree.

-a!-

Ugh.

There's really nothing worse than hyperbole.

-a!-

Two trucks carrying olives collided.

It was quite a kalamata.

-a!-

Interestingly, "Hagen-daz" translates roughly
to: "If you don't know the language, there's no
way you'd know if this claim is true."

-a!-

On a scale of 1 to 10, with 0 being well and 100
being well, how closely do you pay attention?

-a!-

It occurs to me that a superhero with redundant or unnecessary super powers would be called: "Superfluous!"

-a!-

I just got an email with the subject line: "Thank you for your redemption."

Not from a church, as you might expect, but from airmiles.

-a!-

If a question can be answered with: "Frankly my dear, I don't give a damn," then the question was Rhett-orical.

-a!-

Little known fact:

Based on the spatial configuration of an average audience, it's more appropriate to ask for an "oval" of applause.

-a!-

Little known fact about butter:

In France, it's pronounced "boot-ay."

-a!-

Overheard at a school while I was picking up my sons: "I see you have a new English teacher."

"No, he teached me last year."

Time for a refresher perhaps?

-a!-

Dwayne: winner of the "it's not a name, it's a sound effect" award, ten years running.

-a!-

In the sequel to the famous play, Biff also becomes a salesman but leads a double life as a serial killer.

It's called *"Sales of a Deathman."*

-a!-

Shouldn't we start calling failures to lose weight: "waisted opportunities?"

-a!-

In retrospect, perhaps we shouldn't have used a knife to cut the tension.

-a!-

People who believe too strongly in fairy tales are easily *mythled.*

-a!-

A world without cheese would be cheeseless.

Holy cheeseless, would that be terrible!

On a side note, "Holy cheeseless" is now my favourite expression.

-a!-

It's increasingly obvious that the phrase "everything in moderation" has some fairly significant exclusions.

OLD EXPRESSIONS, NEW TWISTS

If you're going through hell, perhaps it's time
to update the GPS.

-a!-

'Tis better to keep one's mouth closed and be
thought a fool, than to open it and incur the
wrath of one's mother-in-law.

-a!-

Wise old saying:

Never have more irons in the fire than wood.

-a!-

What doesn't kill you ... will likely be trying
twice as hard next time.

-a!-

If God really wanted us to stop and smell the
roses more often, He'd have made them smell like
bacon.

-a!-

Personally I prefer the expression "that's just
the cake under the icing".

-a!-

It's all about perspective.

Don't forget, fools says wise men are too
complacent.

-a!-

I disagree. Sometimes, the right word is worth a
thousand pictures.

-a!-

I believe it was Benedict Arnold that said it
best: "Some things happen for a treason."

-a!-

So, apparently weirdness is in the eye of the
beholder as well, if the sour expression on the
face of the old woman behind me in line at the
grocery store is any indication.

-a!-

Granola for breakfast is the most self-important
meal of the day.

-a!-

People who haven't changed since high school
smell horrible.

-a!-

I used to know a kid who was always getting beat
me up because he couldn't keep his mouth shut
and kept offering others his "penny's worth of
advice".

Apparently, his motto was: "In for a penny, in
for a pounding."

-a!-

When one door closes, it's time to hire a
locksmith.

-a!-

And the number one reason people go on holiday:
Because home is no place like there.

-a!-

It occurs to me that the heart wouldn't be as
lonely a hunter if it invited the brain along
occasionally.

-a!-

I'm told to stay humble because our graves are
all the same size, and I'm thinking, isn't the
Great Pyramid just a big grave for, like, one
guy?

-a!-

I took the vacuum outside to clean the car, and
the plants and trees started hurling verbal
abuse at it.

I guess it's true what they say about nature and
vacuums.

-a!-

Dance like nobody's watching but make love like
you've got an audience; it spices things up more
that way.

-a!-

Fortune favours the bold and sometimes the
italic, but never at the same time.

-a!-

A journey of a thousand miles starts and stops
frequently at the mercy of a child's bladder.

-a!-

I'm feeling lazy lately.

Time to start looking for doors of opportunity;
they're easier than the windows.

-a!-

Everything always comes full polygon.

-a!-

An apple a day keeps the doctor away, but only
if you aim for the head.

-a!-

"Who among us can stand the test of time?"

Wait. What?

There's a test at the end of time? I didn't know
that!

-a!-

If I have more than one doctor, should I eat an
apple every day for each one of them?

-a!-

Sure, pressure makes diamonds, but have you seen
what it does to Styrofoam?

-a!-

Pressure makes diamonds eh?

Yeah, it makes hot, explosive geysers too.
What's your point?

-a!-

A journey of a thousand miles usually begins
with an argument over who drives, and often ends
with the realization that you need a better GPS.

-a!-

April showers may bring flowers.

Wait, that's not right.

-a!-

If I were King for just one day, I'd ask about
changing the term limits.

-a!-

Old habits may die hard, but they look so nice
mounted on the wall.

-a!-

I found a bad apple today while making a crisp.

The rest of the apples in the bunch were just
fine.

It might be time to update that tired old
saying.

-a!-

Nine out of ten dentists agree that, when it
comes to some of their procedures, medicine is
the best laughter.

-a!-

If I die before I wake, would I know the
difference?

-a!-

My horse just told me that he's not interested
in having a threesome, and really wishes that
people in the towns we ride into would stop
asking for one.

-a!-

Money can't buy happiness. I guess that's why
all of the people on our currency look so damned
serious.

-a!-

"Old habits die hard," said the Nun who has worn
the same outfit every day for the last thirty
years.

-a!-

Whoever said "if you can't say anything nice,
don't say anything at all" didn't know how
expressive that bitter old woman's silences
can be.

-a!-

Where there's a will, there's a disgruntled,
estranged family member.

-a!-

The long and winding road is difficult one on
which to back up a trailer.

-a!-

SCHRODINGER: LOVE HIM AND/OR HATE HIM.

Interestingly, since most people don't know how
to spell "Schrödinger," to their eyes it is both
correct and incorrect simultaneously.

-a!-

I don't know if my regular mention of
Schrödinger's cat in my posts makes me look
smart, stupid, or both at the same time.

-a!-

Schrödinger's idea that a thing can both exist
and not-exist until a person observes it,
completely falls apart when chocolate is
concerned.

-a!-

Schrödinger's Cup:

Until you roll up the rim and observe what's
underneath, your Timmie's cup is both a winner
AND a loser.

-a!-

"Every hand's a winner, and every hand's a
loser..."

Seems to me that the Gambler giving advice in
the song was Schrödinger in disguise.

-a!-

Schadenfreude's cat:

Until the box is opened, the cat inside it is
both alive and dead, but the observer is hoping
for the worst.

-a!-

Perhaps predictably, friends described
Schrödinger as the kind of guy you either loved
or hated...

-a!-

It's a little known fact that at parties,
Schrödinger would try to pick up women with the
line, "You can't tell, but I may (or may not) be
wearing underwear right now, and the only way to
know for sure is for you to look."

-a!-

When it comes to thinking vs. doing, I believe
it was Schrödinger's cat who famously said,
"Think outside the box all you want, but
nothing's going to happen with me until you
actually do something like opening my box to
take a look."

-a!-

I know I post about Schrödinger a lot, but I'm
not actually sure whether or not I even
completely understand his famous theory about
the cat in the box.

Honestly, it could go either way.

-a!-

LITERARY REFERENCES

Ironically, when books were invented, ancient
adults were concerned that children who read
them would stop using their imagination.

-a!-

Not to be outdone by Harper Lee's new
publication, John Steinbeck is issuing a sequel
to *"Grapes of Wrath"* called *"Raisins of
Conniption"*.

-a!-

I believe it was Gandalf who, when asked for the
wisest thing ever said, replied, "This too shall
not pass."

-a!-

Happy book lovers have a certain joie de livre.

-a!-

Gump meets Seuss:

A person is not what a person was,
A person is what a person does.

-a!-

Imagine my surprise when I read *"Oh the Places
you'll go"* to my kids and discovered that it was
neither about potty training nor toilets.

-a!-

Shakespeare didn't know a thing about physics.

He thought that light could break windows.

-a!-

The "Clapper" never caught on in Neverland.

Every time you'd clap your hands to turn off the lights at night, bright fairies would appear.

-a!-

Dear internets - here's a perfect name for a self-aggrandizing auto-biography: *The Earnesty of Being Important*

You're welcome.

-a!-

Just once I'd like to read a version of *The Grasshopper and the Ant* where the ant learns a valuable lesson about the importance of having fun every once in a while.

-a!-

George R. R. Martin should write a scene in *The Song of Ice and Fire* series where a character asks, "Is life in the kingdom really getting more violent, or are we just hearing about it more?"

-a!-

Writers are turned on by literal stimulation.

-a!-

Literary characters from the same book live in the same neck of the words.

Badum-tish.

-a!-

MADE UP WORDS

ACERBIA:
A suburban neighborhood full of especially bitter people.

AMATEURCRASTINATOR:
Someone who is just learning how to put tasks off until later.

ANONYMOSITY:
An active dislike for people you don't know.

ANATONOMY:
A body part that operates independently of the rest of the body.
See also: **PENIS**.

ANTAGONOSTIC:
Somebody who believes in being openly hostile towards others for what they believe.

DAYSASTER:
A whole day where everything goes absolutely and horribly wrong.

DIMENTIA:
State of serious mental impairment in which a person is no longer able to see depth.

EXCESSERBATION:
The act of playing with yourself far too much.

FELATION:
That happy feeling you get when...
Y'know what? Never mind. My mother and daughter are gonna see this.

FECESCIOUS:
The act treating others like crap, usually with the use of sarcasm.

GREGARIOUS CHANT:
What a person sings when they're feeling particularly sociable.

HIPPOTHESIS:
A large water-loving mammal whose existence has yet to be proven.

HORS GASM
An orgasm in which you have an out of body
experience and go to France.

HYPERBOLIC CHAMBER:
Where a person goes to off-gas an excess of
exaggeration.

HYPNOTHESIS:
A scientific proposition that puts you in a
trance.

INEBREVIATION:
A state when you're drunk, and start talking in
truncated words.

INEXHORRIBLE:
When you know something terrible is about to
happen, and you can't do a thing about it.

INTUITION:
The deep feeling that someday you're going to
have to pay fees for higher learning.

KIDMASTE:
The inner kid in me honours the inner kid in
you.

ORIGASMI:
The ancient art of climaxing while folding the
body into physical arrangements that would make
the Kama Sutra envious.

PHOTOGENETIC:
The scientific reason why beautiful babies run
in a family.

PREPOSAL
If you ask somebody to marry you before they get
the chance to ask you first.

RECTALACTIVELY:
Doing something using hindsight.

REVERSE-ENGIQUEERING:
The act of trying to out somebody as Gay after
they're dead.

SADOMATHOCHIST:
Somebody who derives pleasure from puzzling out
frustrating number-based problems.

SCHADENFROIDE:
Deriving a sick sense of pleasure in watching a
francophone shiver uncomfortably in the cold.

SELF-DEFECATING:
Talking about yourself in an extremely unkind,
derogatory way.

SEQUESTION:
When someone makes an inquiry from isolation.

SOLIPSTICE:
A seasonal change that happens only to the self.

SOLIPLIPSTICK:
The theory that nothing else exists while you're
fixing your makeup.
See also: **DANGEROUS DRIVING HABITS**.

STATIC ECCENTRICITY:
Stationary objects that don't stay put because
they're behaving in an erratic, off-center
manner.

TEAMERITY:
Making a group effort to be bold and audacious.

TEN-TO-NINE-US:
A gloomy sense of despondency that hits you at
8:50 in the morning, when you realize that
another work day is about to begin, and there's
not a bloody thing you can do about it.

UNNOVATION:
A new feature on a product that makes NO
improvement to it whatsoever.

YOUTHANIZE:
To be injected with a youthful energy.
"I've been youthanized, and I feel like a kid
again!"

VOYEURAGEUR:
A canoeist who likes to watch.

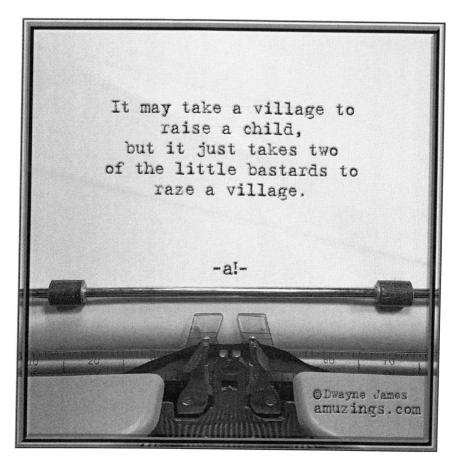

It may take a village to
raise a child,
but it just takes two
of the little bastards to
raze a village.

-a!-

©Dwayne James
amuzings.com

ACERBIC EXERCISE
Posts with a Little Bit of an Edge

Where others start their morning with a little
aerobic exercise, I prefer to get a little
acerbic exercise instead.

-a!-

I can't help but notice that people complaining
about modern technology aren't doing it through
the use of homing pigeons.

-a!-

Of course I'm in love with myself, but it's not
like we're being exclusive.

-a!-

I've learned to stop asking "is it just me"
questions because I've come to conclusion that
it usually is.

-a!-

How did the expression "There are no original
ideas" come into being?

The first time it was said it would have been an
original idea, and therefore it should have
vanished in a puff of logic.

-a!-

Ah, life in the country.

Where the internet and the water pressure
compete for the title of *Most Sluggish.*

-a!-

Apparently, in French, the name for the
"convenience" tabs on bottles translates
literally to:"Fuck you. Use a knife."

-a!-

It seems to me that our parents severely
overestimated the threat posed by groups of
friends collectively jumping off bridges.

-a!-

I only regret that the 140 character limit
didn't allow me to pepper my previous tweet with
the kind and variety of curse words it deserved.

-a!-

I only regret that I have but one fuck to give,
and I'm saving it for something truly
outrageous.

-a!-

Wow. Interference, elbowing, and fake injuries.

If the House of Commons gets any more like
hockey, we'll need a Don Cherry commentary.

-a!-

Note to self: most women do not find it amusing
when you call attention to their flatulence by
saying, "Pardon me. Did you say something?"

-a!-

Manipulative political attack ads are especially
effective on those same users who fall for
Facebook hoaxes.

This means that we're living at a time when our
leaders are chosen by the same people who think
that Mark Zuckerberg pays for shared posts.

-a!-

Perhaps predictably, those who are trying to
organize a boycott of social media are having a
hard time getting the word out.

-a!-

A woman should never have to say, "My eyes are
up here." Especially to her optometrist.

-a!-

We all have that one friend who does something
batshit crazy and then says, "Well, in my
defense, you did hold my beer."

-a!-

Let he (or she) who is without drama flip the
first board game.

-a!-

As a writer, I've always wanted to move people
with my words.

So if you would be so kind as to get up and walk
around, I'd appreciate it.

-a!-

You can catch a lot more flies with a bowl of
feces on the counter, but some people just
aren't ready for that level of commitment.

-a!-

When the online ad claimed to be able to offer
"significant growth", I honestly didn't think it
was referring to my credit card bill.

-a!-

I read an article the other day that claimed
that people only read headlines these days.

OK, so I didn't read the whole article, but I'm
pretty sure it made a valid point.

-a!-

I see the snap judgements are blossoming this
morning, but I'm going to wait until they ripen
into informed opinions before I harvest any.

-a!-

They say never to go to bed angry, but last night I was furious at how exhausted I was and how late I stayed up, so I never went to bed.

-a!-

I'm feeling kinda lazy today and don't feel like standing up, so I think I'll just be sitting corrected if that's OK with everyone.

-a!-

My biggest fear is dying alone.

Mostly because I've given my last words a lot of thought, and it would be a shame if nobody was there to hear them.

-a!-

That is one magical marketing genius who has been able to sell the idea that the solution to the problem of too many guns is more guns.

-a!-

I'm concerned that children's literature is giving our children the impression that old ladies swallow a lot of ridiculous things.

-a!-

I think I'm supposed to be offended by something you said, but I'm going to have to go online to see why and by how much.

-a!-

I've decided that my first tattoo will read: "I regret this tattoo already".

-a!-

I go to the YMCA during the day because there
just aren't enough wrinkled old naked men around
if I exercise at home.

-a!-

Never take advice to let your freak flag fly
from the same source that makes fun of freaky
flag-flying people.

I'm looking at you social media.

-a!-

The YES side in the Scottish independence vote
missed an opportunity: the best way to break up
a British group is to get Yoko Ono involved.

-a!-

Flattened chickens.

Because simply slaughtering an animal, cutting
it up, and wrapping it in plastic wasn't nearly
humiliating enough.

-a!-

I never burn bridges. At least not immediately.

I pack all my bridges with dynamite after
crossing them so that I can destroy them later.

-a!-

Every time I take the compost out and struggle
to pry the frikkin' lid off the composter, I
remind myself to ask the raccoon how he does it.

-a!-

The claim, that anything repeated enough becomes
true is a lie that's been repeated so much that
it's become true.

-a!-

Apparently, there are only two foods known to
never rot: honey and the McDonald's Happy Meal.

-a!-

"You're my shelter from troubled winds," she
said as she squeezed my hand. "And, sometimes,
you're the source of those troubled winds."

-a!-

Out for a birthday supper and the waitress asked
if I had a "Senior" card.

Turns out she said "Scene" card and we laughed
and laughed even as I tried to ask how much I
could have saved.

-a!-

The *Honey Nut Cheerios* cereal is proof that you
can put honey on anything and make it taste
good, even tiny pieces of cardboard.

-a!-

Similar to the UV index, the internet should
warn you as to the level of sanctimony you can
be prepared to experience on any given day.

-a!-

When my kids ask what life was like in the 70s,
I say, "It was a time when unattractive people
were allowed to make music and star on TV cop
shows."

-a!-

Like polio, passive aggressiveness had all but
been eradicated from the world by the end of the
20th century.

But then Facebook came along...

-a!-

If we can legislate what is printed on cigarette
packages to discourage their purchase, why don't
we just make lit cigarettes smell like farts?

-a!-

Where I appreciate your unsolicited opinion, I
only take online advice from celebrities.

-a!-

I've decided that, from now on, I will only
believe in things I can see.

So, sorry fish, I no longer believe in you, and
I'm iffy on chameleons.

-a!-

I'd be offended by your accusation that I have a
short attention span had I not stopped listening
to you like ten minutes ago.

-a!-

I'm not sure if our neighbour is cutting his
lawn or flying a small noisy helicopter around
his yard.

-a!-

Oh puh-lease. I don't need religion to tell me
what's right and wrong. I've got social media
for that.

-a!-

You call it "radio news." I call it "tiny voice
in the distance I can barely hear because kids."

-a!-

This bag of chocolate chips is resealable.

How quaint.

Like I'm actually going to use that feature.
Like, ever.

-a!-

Isn't it ironic to join a SOCIAL network and
expect privacy?

Isn't that like going to a party and telling
people that you're not really there?

-a!-

The problem with democracy is that too many
people don't know what's good for them, and the
rest only think they do.

-a!-

When I'm Santa, I will charge kids an indulgence
to be put on the nice list.

I figure if the Catholic Church can do it, why
not Santa.

-a!-

The biggest hoax in society today isn't rigged elections or climate change, it's radio stations who claim to play "whatever".

-a!-

I'm just saying that if this radio station really was playing "whatever", I'd be hearing the occasional show tune.

-a!-

Adult cough syrup would be a lot more palatable if they made it in flavours like: "Baileys," or "Single malt."

-a!-

After 170 years, Franklin's lost ship, HMS Terror was found in *Terror Bay.*

May I recommend we look for Amelia Earhart on *Amelia Island?*

-a!-

Not being able to cook pancakes directly on the surface of a flat top stove seems like a wasted opportunity to me.

-a!-

I love it when a Facebook friend I kinda knew in high school posts a pic of themselves as a kid, and I'm like, "Oh, THAT'S who you are."

-a!-

I've never liked people making plans for me.

It's probably one of the reasons I don't like organized religion.

-a!-

If a person has forgotten more about something
than I know about it, I'd be more concerned
about their senility than my competence.

-a!-

Got a tea in one hand and a paint brush in the
other and neither one is asking for a password.

-a!-

For the last time, *fatuous* has nothing to do
with weight, *pedagogy* is not sexual deviance,
and *niggardly* isn't a racial slur.

We good now?

-a!-

As much as I want to read your post, it's got an
awful lot of words in it.

I've already read a lot of words today.

-a!-

Why did I get so many grapes?

Well, A, they were on sale, and B, I was
concerned that our fruit flies were underfed.

-a!-

I never know which celebrity deaths to care
about until the Oscar's *"In Memorian"* when I can
hear who gets more applause.

-a!-

How do I tell this customer survey that the best
way they can keep me happy as a customer is to
stop asking me to take customer surveys?

-a!-

If the psychic in my dream last night really did
know my future, then shouldn't she have known
the alarm was about to interrupt her?

-a!-

As a kid, I was lousy at "Barrel of Monkeys"
yet, now, I can pull three or four hangers out
of the closet at a time with no effort at all.

-a!-

There are some days when you just know ahead of
time that you're going to be needing an extra
layer of tinfoil in your hat.

-a!-

I'm pretty sure that singing a *Michael Bolton*
song out loud isn't a symptom of a stroke, but
it probably should be.

-a!-

Now I'm normally not one to judge, but I'm a
little concerned that my neighbour's primary
pastime is coming outside to watch her dog poo.

-a!-

I'm pretty sure that "Bluetooth" is French for,
"Naw. I'm just not feeling it today. Try me
tomorrow."

-a!-

Apparently, we have things in the kitchen whose
only purpose is to fall out onto the floor when
we open cupboards.

-a!-

Facebook.

Where a post in support of mental health is
followed by a meme joking that meds are the only
thing keeping the poster from killing people.

-a!-

If the Super Bowl ever starts to fly around and
fight crime, then I'll start watching it.

Until then: *Meh.*

-a!-

I'm being told that my acerbic comments from the
kitchen, although hilarious, are not helping the
boys with their homework.

-a!-

The reason Trump's tweets run contrary to what
his advisor's tell him is because his thumbs
aren't opposable, they're oppositional defiant.

-a!-

Apparently, the update to the Clue board game
will be called "Clueless."

All players will be on smartphones and won't
know or care about the murder.

-a!-

Most excellent book Mr. Vonnegut. Now, where can
I get *Slaughterhouse* books *1* to *4?*

-a!-

If you think gravity sucks, then you grossly
misunderstand one of the fundamental physical
forces of the universe.

-a!-

And, in a surprise move today, the *Society for
the Prevention of Cruelty to Animals* charged
curiosity for killing all those cats.

-a!-

Die you then and happens shit, but not always in
that order.

-a!-

My goal today is to be just half as great as I
claim to be on Facebook.

-a!-

I flossed tonight.

So, if I understand the rules, that means I
don't have to do it again until the eve of my
next dentist appointment, about six months from
now.

Right?

-a!-

May the 4th is coming.

That means everyone who mocked me for loving
Star Wars as a kid will soon be greeting me like
we're suddenly family.

-a!-

Social media conundrum:

I really agree with a post and want to share it, but it's got a glaring spelling and/or grammatical mistake, and I can't be associated with that shit.

-a!-

"Describe yourself with one word," she said.

"Rule breaker," he answered.

"That's two words."

"Exactly."

-a!-

The lunatics aren't running the asylum yet, but they do appear to have taken control of all the exits.

-a!-

I'm about to replace a broken light socket, and the instructions say to throw the breaker first.

OK. What's a breaker, and where do I throw it?

If anything goes wrong, I'm blaming the instructions.

-a!-

This bacon is sliced so thin that it's more like a veneer.

-a!-

You miss the good old days?

You mean back when hospitals had smoking sections and kids sang about catching something by the toe that wasn't a tiger?

-a!-

I'm sure that, were he alive today, he would say that he doesn't like to be quoted posthumously.

-a!-

Those who think that it's an honour just to be nominated don't realize how many major awards let you nominate yourself.

-a!-

It's funny how incompetence and incontinence sorta sound the same, and both involve having to clean up somebody else's crap.

-a!-

Every once in a while I think about taking up jogging. But then my knees speak up and say, "You're going to put this to a vote first right?"

-a!-

Apparently, I like to digress.

Let me tell you a story about how I came to this realization...

-a!-

Every Christmas season, it irks me that we're changing traditional terminology.

Sure, "snowthrower" is more accurate but it will ALWAYS be a snowblower to me.

-a!-

There are two kinds of people who irritate me:

1. People who make lists.

b). People who switch from numbered to lettered
bullets in the middle of those lists.

-a!-

Forty days and forty nights in a confined space
with only eight people to clean up after
thousands of animals.

I'd say the unicorns got off easy.

-a!-

Why do some psychics need you to make an
appointment? Shouldn't they already know when
you're coming?

And why do you have to cancel when something
comes up?

-a!-

I'll consider going to a Psychic Fair the day I
get a "Thank You for Attending" Card from them
ahead of time.

-a!-

Respectfully, before I go tying any yellow
ribbons on our oak tree, just what was it you
were in prison for?

-a!-

What do we want: IRONY!

When do we want it: WE ALREADY HAVE IT!

-a!-

It occurs to me that we could save ourselves a
bundle in long term health care costs by simply
moving the outdoor smoking sections even further
away from our buildings like, say to the middle
of busy intersections.

-a!-

Other men my age fantasize about renting an
apartment downtown for their mistress.

Me? I fantasize about renting a room downtown
with reliable internet.

-a!-

With respect to *Folgers*, I always thought that
the best part of waking up was not being dead.

-a!-

What'd we do before the internet?

Mostly, we listened to our parents drone on and
on about how the TV was destroying meaningful
human interaction.

-a!-

"There's more to life than sex?"

Really? Where do they think life comes from?

-a!-

I wonder if that couple from the *Pina Colada*
song is still together.

Seems to me that they might have had some trust
issues.

-a!-

I've finally reached that point in my career
when I'm ready for my duet album.

-a!-

The joke's on you Sir.

Singing faux-opera loudly while in public IS my
day job.

-a!-

Y'know, I really want to take the high road
here, but I get nosebleeds easily.

-a!-

Actually, necessity is the mother of a lot of
things.

She's very fertile and gets around.

-a!-

I'm so bad at sarcasm that I call it "suckasm".

-a!-

I think I speak for everyone when I say that I
hate when somebody tries to put words in my
mouth.

-a!-

July actually has another, more popular name.

Think about it.

Just ask anyone what month it is during the
actual month of July, and they'll answer with:
JulyAlready.

-a!-

That self-righteous feeling when you walk into
Tim's past a long drive-thru line, get a coffee,
and walk out again to see the same people still
sitting in their cars, not having moved.

-a!-

That self-righteous feeling you get when you
park your car in the lot one business over from
Tim's so you don't get trapped in your car in
the parking lot by their drive-thru line.

-a!-

The newer "jet engine" style hand dryers in
public washrooms really drive the point home
that the old ones were about as effective as
blowing on your hands yourself.

-a!-

My kids often ask me what life was like in my
youth.

I answer that it was sitting on the toilet
without your phone or tablet to keep you
company.

-a!-

Let him or her who has not committed a minor
traffic infraction lift the first middle finger.

-a!-

I'm told I should live every moment like it's my
last.

So, from now on, I will continuously scream, "I
don't want to die!"

-a!-

When I was renewing my Health card today, the
lady confirmed with me that I was an organ donor
and then asked me to go behind the curtain in
the corner.

"Why? Do you want them now?" I asked.

I suspect I'm gonna have a funny expression in
the pictures she took of me behind that curtain.

-a!-

Strong opinions are like farts.

You probably shouldn't share them openly with
people you've just met.

-a!-

Saying, "It's 2016, why is this still a thing?"
is sooooo 2001.

-a!-

The Martians used to think the economy was more
important than the environment too.

Look what happened to them.

-a!-

I was having an amazing dream and asked a friend
in the dream to pinch me.

He did and it woke me up.

Next time I see him, I'm gonna punch him in the
head.

-a!-

Hey Sting, sending a thousand marriage proposals
a day is harassment, even if it is done in "some
old fashioned way."

-a!-

I don't like apps that show me content based
solely on my previous choices. It's like saying
"We've analyzed the keyboard keys you use most
often, and are taking the rest away."

-a!-

If it's true that we become what we complain
about, then I should tell you that my good looks
are getting way out of hand.

-a!-

ON SINGLE FRIENDS WITH NO KIDS...

On days my kids are raging lunatics, I just love
reading posts from single friends asking who's
free to see movies, or concerts, or plays.

-a!-

My single friend posted that she can't decide
what book to read next today.

Meanwhile, my kids just lost their minds because
I switched their pillows.

-a!-

"Best wine for a quiet evening and a good book?"
my single friend just posted.

Meanwhile, I wanna know the best cleanser to
gets kid's puke out of carpet. Keep in mind, my
son had birthday cake with bright red icing with
supper. You do the math.

-a!-

Asking for a friend:

When your single friend posts that he "couldn't
get out of bed this morning," is "Fuck you" an
appropriate response?

-a!-

THE END
I hope you enjoyed your read!

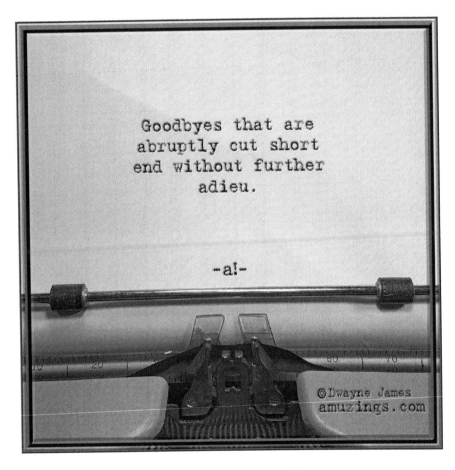

Goodbyes that are
abruptly cut short
end without further
adieu.

-a!-

©Dwayne James
amuzings.com

ABOUT THE AUTHOR

Watercolour artist and author Dwayne James lives outside Lakefield, Ontario where he writes and paints as often as he can, that is when he's not spending time with his very forgiving family.

Dwayne has a Master's Degree in archaeology, something he claims is definitive proof that he knows how to write creatively. "Indeed, the most important skill I learned in university," he posits, "was the ability to pretentiously write about myself in the third person."

After spending close to a decade as a technical writer at a large computer company, Dwayne opted to look at their decision to downsize him as an opportunity to become a stay@home Dad for his newborn twins and pursue his painting and writing whenever the boys allowed.

It is a decision that continues to make him giggle with wild abandon to this very day.

VISIT DWAYNE ONLINE:

His personal Web page:
www.dwaynerjames.com

His virtual art studio and store:
www.resteddy.com.

His Facebook page:
http://www.facebook.com/dwaynerjames

His Smashwords page:
https://www.smashwords.com/profile/view/dwaynerjames

The official *amuzings* Web page:
www.amuzings.com

The official *amuzings* Facebook page:
https://www.facebook.com/amuzings

25376194R10124

Made in the USA
Columbia, SC
03 September 2018